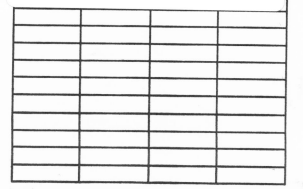

KATY PERRY

ife of
eworks

Exclusive Distributors:

MUSIC SALES LIMITED
14/15 Berners Street, London. W1T 3LJ.
United Kingdom.

MUSIC SALES CORPORATION
257 Park Avenue South, New York. NY 10010.
United States of America.

MACMILLAN DISTRIBUTION SERVICES
56 Parkwest Drive, Derrimut. Vic 3030.
Australia.

Every effort has been made to trace the copyright holders of
the photographs in this book but one or two were unreachable.
We would be grateful if the photographers concerned would contact us.
Printed in the E.U.
A catalogue record for this book is available from the British Library.
Visit Omnibus Press at www.omnibuspress.com

KATY

PERRY

A Life of
Fireworks
CHLOE GOVAN

OMNIBUS PRESS

For Steve
In Loving Memory

Contents

Acknowledgments

Thanks go to interviewees Printz Board, Russ Breimeier, Mike Caffrey, Agatha Carubia, Mandy Collinger-Parsons, Rich Davis, DeWayne Hamby, David Henley, Nathan Kreitzer, Adam LaClave, Mark Moring, Jill Sobule, Carol Thomas, John J. Thompson, Matthew Turner, Brian White, Philip Von Wrede and all the additional, anonymous interviewees who participated.

Chapter 1

Talking In Tongues

It's no easy feat winning over a deeply repressed, devoutly religious Christian audience in the heart of America's Bible belt – least of all for a scantily clad preacher's daughter tottering on the stage in four-inch high stilettos and clutching a lipstick-shaped inflatable phallus. Yet Katy was a woman willing to take on the challenge – and she wasn't nearly finished yet. As waves of shock rippled through the audience, she briefly but passionately locked lips with a female member of the crowd for good measure. Alongside the occasional boo were deafening roars of approval. Katy was breaking down society's last taboos and all with a deceptively innocent smile – she had kissed a girl and she'd loved it. To more conservative viewers, the scene was unspeakably shocking, but for Katy it was just another day in her life on the stage.

From a shy teenage tomboy who'd never heard chart music and lived in baggy sweaters to a flirtatious glamour puss penning songs that had pastors everywhere shaking their heads in righteous indignation, Katy had made quite a transformation. Yet where had it all begun?

Katy was born to Mary Perry, a mixed-race globetrotter of German and Portuguese descent, and husband Keith Hudson, an all-American Memphis-born preacher, on October 25, 1984, and christened Kathryn Elizabeth. The one thing both her parents had in common was a commitment to a devout religious lifestyle – and that was a priority they passed on to Katy. From the very beginning, her life was one of rules, boundaries and restrictions. "I knew about Hell from the moment I understood a sentence," she told *Rolling Stone*. "I had fuzzy felt boards with Satan and people gnashing their teeth." In her early years, MTV and even VH1 were permanently blocked from the family TV set to protect Katy from catching a glimpse of dirty dancing. Secular music and movies were banned for their atheist outlook and she was even forbidden from eating processed sugar.

"My religious upbringing was comically strict – even the Dirt Devil vacuum cleaner was banned," Katy later revealed to *Rolling Stone*. "In our house, no-one was allowed to refer to devilled eggs. We had to call them angelic eggs. We were never allowed to swear. I'd get into trouble just for saying 'Hell, no!' If you dropped a hammer on your toe in our house, you had to say something like 'Jiminy Christmas.'"

She continued: "I wasn't ever able to say I was lucky because my mother would rather us say that we were blessed and she also didn't like that lucky sounded like Lucifer. I wasn't allowed to eat Lucky Charms, but I think that was the sugar. I think my mom lied to me about that one."

Talking of how her parents had censored all non-Christian influences, Katy told *CBS News*: "You know, there was a movie called *Jesus Camp* and I watched it and I was like 'Oh my God!' I didn't know they had behind the scenes footage of my childhood!'"

Jesus Camp was a 2006 documentary that lifted the lid on the controversial world of a children's strict Christian summer camp in North Dakota. According to the founders of the camp, their aim was to train young children as young as five as miniature warriors for God's army and to encourage them to "take America back for Christ".

In the film, founder Becky Fischer warns a group of terrified children that if mythical storybook wizard Harry Potter had existed in Biblical times, "he would have been put to death". Meanwhile, another scene sees youngsters reprimanded with the words, "A lot of you say you're Christians but how many of you are leading separate lives?" The pastor then invites the increasingly hysterical group of pre-teen children to "clean up their act" while she pours a bottle of water into their outstretched hands to purge their sins.

Children were filmed sobbing in repentance, begging for forgiveness and even joining anti-abortion campaigns with red Sellotape depicting the word "Life" sealing their mouths shut. Later, the same children were encouraged to take a hammer and smash cups emblazoned with the word "Government" – an institution the camp is allegedly trying to overthrow.

According to Fischer, democracy is undesirable as it gives non-believers and sinners equal freedom. Dancing was forbidden at the camp and even ghost stories were denounced as "dishonourable to God". Was the camp craving a Christian jihad, a full-scale religious war?

The motivation of the group's leaders was to overthrow the government and outwit the "enemy", Islam. America responded with indignation and outrage. The Richard Dawkins Foundation posted a ridiculing critique on its website, entitled Surviving Jesus Camp. It raged "Forget *Texas Chainsaw Massacre* – if you're looking for a horror movie, Fischer is enough to scare the crap out of you, this woman who would get off by putting a made-up kid wizard to the stake... No point voting on gay rights, when the Bible says it's bad, no point voting on abortion when the Bible says it's murder. The Bible, not democracy, has all the answers. This is sharia law by another name – and whatever your views on these issues, it is scary."

One blogger concurred, "In this moment, we see not only the power behind religion's throne but the roots of Nazism, Soviet enslavement and terrorism. Imagine being in kindergarten and hearing that you are vile and need to confess your sins to the Lord!"

Meanwhile another raged, "If there is one thing which *Jesus Camp* reveals, it is the extent to which some adults will rob children of a normal childhood in order to foster their own politico-religious agenda. The children in this film are not being inculcated with moral and spiritual values – they are being manipulated into quasi-religious hysteria. This isn't faith – it's hypnosis."

The camp stood accused of rewriting stories of the Big Bang with creationist theories, and using God's words to teach everything from moral studies to geometry. Some Christian websites defended the documentary, calling it "powerful", "profound" and "inspiring". Yet to many, it was a sinister cult that controlled children by "brainwashing" them with a guilt they were too young to understand. Meanwhile for Katy, some of the scenes were just a part of everyday life.

She shared the uncertainty of a 10-year-old at the camp who adored Christian music but was fearful of her urge to dance, not for God but "for the flesh" – the sheer enjoyment of it. The girl earnestly informs others at the camp that the desire to dance can be overcome with "effort and concentration".

Katy too was encouraged to listen exclusively to religious songs and was told that secular tunes were "the devil's music". Obvious candidates such as Madonna, who had prostrated herself on a cross, were banned from the house but even seemingly innocent boy bands such as New Kids On The Block were on the reject list. "I was raised in a very pseudo-religious household where the only thing on the menu was gospel standards like 'Oh Happy Day', 'His Eye Is On The Sparrow' and 'Amazing Grace' – all eight verses of it," Katy chuckled to *MTV*.

Yet somehow Katy found access to the occasional illicit pop tune – and, what was more, she lacked the discipline of the young girl on the documentary. She confessed to *Prefix* magazine, "*Jagged Little Pill* [by Alanis Morissette] was huge for me. One of the vivid memories of my childhood is swinging on the swing set singing 'Ironic' at the top of my lungs. I went to a Christian school, so I got into a little trouble for that one!"

It wasn't just secular music that *Jesus Camp* saw as harmful, but mainstream TV shows and movies as well. The film depicted the camp's founder throwing a magnetic hand on to a plastic model of a person's brain and watching it stick. The message was that popular culture eroded spirituality and stained a child's mind long after the film was over. Unfortunately for Katy, her parents felt exactly the same.

"There was only church," she recalled to *Sunday Times Style*. "Church friends, church school and of course, actual church. I thought it was normal at the time, but it wasn't. I could only go to the movies if they reviewed it first. They let me see anything with a remnant of God –

Sister Act 2, The Preacher's Wife, that kinda thing." H
PG13 movies at their discretion while R-rated m
forbidden. Meanwhile those without a Christian
the cut at all. Even fictional cartoon characters v
Christian. For the children of *Jesus Camp* it was Harry Potter and
Katy it was *The Smurfs*.

Katy also related to the camp's depiction of talking in tongues. The
scenes of young children writhing on the floor and communicating with
the spirit might have seemed horrifying to some, but for Katy, that too
was a familiar part of growing up. The Richard Dawkins Foundation
reviewed: "With arms in the air, they are instructed on how to let the
spirit take over their bodies and speak in tongues. The children imitate.
Many of them cry. Some fall to the ground and shake on the floor in what
looks like an epileptic seizure. More cry. This all looked very unhealthy...
these adults, no matter what their intentions, were performing horrific
acts of mental child abuse." The scene was denounced as "unforgivable"
and led the film website *Cinema Blend* to describe it as a contender for
"the most chilling horror movie of the year".

Yet Katy remembered her own experiences of talking in tongues
more fondly. She told *Rolling Stone*, "My mom and dad practise
tongues and interpretation together – my dad speaks in tongues, my
mom interprets it. Speaking in tongues is as normal to me as 'Pass the
salt.'" She added: "A lot of religions use meditation or chanting as a
subliminal prayer language and speaking in tongues isn't that different
– it's a secret, direct language to God. If I felt intuitively that I had to
pray for some situation, but I didn't rationally understand it, I just let
my spirit pray for it."

Whether *Jesus Camp* was encouraging children to lay their lives down
for the Gospel, and controlling and manipulating followers by posing
as an extension of God, or whether their intentions were sincere, the
controversy became too much for its creators. Shortly after the film
debuted and the protests began, the camp closed its doors to the public
indefinitely.

Yet Katy's life of obedience to God continued. Until the age of
three, she lived in the sleepy coastal village of Goleta, California. Just a

v miles away from hedonistic Santa Barbara, it had a more laid-back atmosphere. Katy appreciated the "peaceful island paradise" surrounded by surfers, sunbathers and holiday-makers – for her, it was no holiday but her everyday world.

Yet her life was turned upside down when her parents embarked on a state-by-state tour of the country, setting up evangelical churches wherever they went. They settled briefly each time before hitting the road again, leaving Katy without roots. "We moved a lot because my dad was an evangelist," she recalled. "We lived in two different places in Oklahoma, then two places in Arizona and then Florida for a while, then back to Santa Barbara – you can take a breath now! I think at the time it affected me emotionally because I had to leave friends so often that I thought I would never make more friends like the ones I left behind. But looking back, I got to make a lot of friends, see a lot of places and take a little bit of everywhere with me."

The family gave their all to God and at times were desperately poor. "Sometimes, we ate from the same food bank we used to feed our congregation," Katy told *Rolling Stone*. The family could not even afford healthcare. By the time she finally visited a dentist as an adult, she needed 13 fillings – more than half of her teeth were covered in cavities.

Meanwhile her parents preached, gave regular sermons and claimed to be able to heal the sick using the power of the Holy Spirit. Underneath their devout exterior, however, Katy's parents were hiding some secrets of their own. Both had lived a fast-paced party lifestyle in the past that had nearly killed them. Katy's mother had been a world traveller before settling in Zimbabwe and briefly marrying, following an ill-fated love affair. She had even dated the guitarist Jimi Hendrix in the seventies.

Meanwhile Katy's father had abandoned his Tennessee roots to live the life of a West Coast socialite. He quickly befriended the counter-cultural drug enthusiast Timothy Leary, who introduced him to his first hit of LSD. Katy told *The Mirror* later: "My mother used to hang out with Jimi Hendrix and my father sold acid called Strawberry Fields for Timothy Leary. Even though my mum isn't the wild child rock 'n' roller pot smoking debutant that she was and my dad isn't the acid dealer with long hair any more, they've probably had more intense moments than anything I've ever done."

To the young Katy, a lifestyle of sex, drugs and rock 'n' roll was infinitely more appealing than her own sheltered Christian upbringing and she would plead with her mother as an adult: "Mom, you shouldn't have been such a prude with [Jimi] – I would have been a Hendrix!"

However, there was a dark side to her parents' hedonism and Katy feared that if they hadn't turned to religion, they might not have survived the phase. "Dad would have died from one tab too many," she told *The Daily Telegraph*. "They both had a wild life, then they found God and felt like they needed to have a personal change and that's how they decided to raise me." At the same time as finding salvation, Keith and Mary had found each other – and Katy's destiny as a preacher's child was set.

Despite her parents' colourful history, there would be no rock 'n' roll sleepovers for Katy, who in the early days wasn't allowed to so much as chastely kiss a boy, let alone a girl. They had lived a lifestyle where partying had been their only religion, but now, seeing Jesus as their saviour, they wanted to protect Katy from making the same mistakes.

Katy's life couldn't have been much less like rock 'n' roll, with many weekends spent antique hunting. "From the age of eight, my dad would wake me up early on a Saturday morning and we'd go to garage sales or to the house of someone who'd recently passed away whose family were selling everything," she explained to *The Daily Mail*. "I'd find a purple glass doorknob from the twenties and it would be going for a song. I have a good eye. I [was] just drawn to old well-made stuff that had its own personality."

As a child however, this life could become mundane. Desperate to break the tedium, Katy sought ways to brighten things up and get the attention she had longed for. She committed her first sin against God when she developed a taste for beauty pageants. The Bible urged its readers not to judge on outward appearance, insisting: "Look not on [someone's] countenance or on the height of his stature, because I have refused him; for the Lord seeth not as man seeth; for man looketh on the outward appearance, but the Lord looketh on the heart." Despite this warning, an increasingly vanity-prone Katy was determined to be the best. The family had been living in Lake Havasu, Arizona at the time, when her mother – also thrilled by the attention – entered her daughter into a mini-pageant held at a grocery store.

Katy later blogged: "It wasn't a hard race – just between a couple of other girls at the store." Yet she earned a "measly" second place. She later competed in a real pageant, but was equally disappointed the second time around. "I got second place [again]," she blogged. "SECOND PLACE IS NOT GOOD ENOUGH... I bet it was because Mom cut corners – took her own pictures, over-Swarovski a jacket or something. Actually, you could probably not ever OVER-Swarovski ANYTHING in a Little Miss Perfect pageant!" she joked. The competitive nature of the game was to stay with her for years to come.

Still keen to be the apple of the nation's eye, she added as an adult: "OK, maybe there's an age restriction. That's fine, I'll just become a pageant mom. I'm sure there's room for two pageant bitches. Soft curls, fake lashes, crystals and a big smile, welcome to your Little Miss Perfect addiction!"

Katy's parents had proudly taken several photographs of her in action, including one of her wearing a pink satin suit and matching bowler hat, her naturally strawberry blonde hair and a broad smile.

However, ultimately, netting the runner's up prize didn't achieve the level of drama that she'd been hoping for and Katy abandoned pageants and went back to the drawing board. As a middle child, she constantly strived for attention, hoping to outdo her younger brother and copy her older sister.

"I was a hyperactive kid," she told *The Daily Mail*, "and my mom and dad got used to me creating a stir. Whether we were on holiday or eating around the dining table, I would always come up with something outrageous."

Katy also committed another sin at the tender age of nine – praying to her creator for immodestly large breasts. "I remember really vividly kneeling by my bed, saying my prayers and asking God to give me boobs that were so big that if I laid on my back, I wouldn't be able to see my feet," she told *Blender* magazine.

Several years later, her prayers were granted – but at her peril. By 13, she'd been punished for her un-Christian request to the point that she longed for a surgical reduction. "I had really bad back problems," she added. "Then I grew up and lost the baby fat and said, 'Hey, this isn't all that bad.'"

Failing with pageantry, she embarked on a new mission – to be even more boyish than her brother. She would frequently come home "battered and bruised" from exploits outside climbing trees, jumping off high ledges and surfing or skateboarding. She had turned herself into a tomboy. Her brother Daniel told *E! Entertainment*, "Katy was like a brother to me, because she was just so rugged and didn't care."

She quickly developed a short-lived passion for skateboarding but gave it up when she feared for her safety. "I spent all day at the skateboard park with a friend of mine who was so good that she ended up going pro," she told *The Daily Mail*. "I wasn't quite so good, but I could easily handle a half pipe, when you're skateboarding almost vertically. I gave it up because I was scuffing my knees so much and I didn't like the idea of breaking bones."

Not only that, but her attempts to win attention failed, eliciting little more than tuts of disapproval from her now straight-laced parents. It was then that she found the ultimate way to get instant love and attention – and that power lay in her voice. "When I would sing, people's faces would light up," she told the *Oregonian*. "It was my only magic trick."

It had all started with a gospel track Katy had come across by chance and sung along with to imitate her sister. "I picked up a Carman track," she told *Christian Music Central*. "That's honest. 'River Of Life' by Carman. That's all I ever grew up on, Christian music. I picked it up because my sister started singing and I copied every little thing she did. It was actually her tape but I stole it. So I took it and I practised it and I performed it before she did."

To her surprise, her parents warmed to the idea of her singing and suggested she take lessons with a voice coach. Eager for approval,

Katy agreed. Yet at first it was her mother who encouraged the then reluctant girl to take her talent further and practise what she had learnt in church. "Mom was actually the first one to get me involved in this," Katy admitted to *Christian Retailing*. "She threw me off the edge because she's a total stage mom! Then I came back and realised this is what I want to do, not what my parents want me to do. It's likewise with my faith, forever with my parents. I just adopted it on my own. And basically I've adopted music as my own."

She added, "My mom would take me when I was 11 or so and we'd do [concerts at] weekend churches. I didn't want to be there because I wanted to be 11. I wanted to do what you do at 11. But then I saw how I affected and touched people [with my voice]."

Before long she was making vision boards with her classmates at school – a motivational exercise to record where children wanted to be in the future – and taping pictures of teenage singers with trophies on them. She now knew she wanted to make it big in music some day.

Katy also enjoyed the prestige that came with being the only musical one. "Nobody in my family can hold a pitch – it's so funny. They really try but they really can't," she told *Cross Rhythms*. "I don't really know where it came from. I think it was just because I was bored and wanted to get into something. Plus, because I'm a middle child, I needed to get attention."

No longer fighting for recognition, Katy was rewarded with $10 by her father each time she sang. She would appear on stage at church, at family functions and even for birthday meals in restaurants when she would serenade the table with the latest gospel tune. "Wherever I went, restaurants or whatever, I would get up and sing 'Amazing Grace'," Katy later revealed to *The Mail*. "Not that I was one of those stage kids. There was no JonBenét Ramsey inside of me waiting to burst out. I just started... writing little songs about God or this boy I liked, the two men in my life at the same time."

It embarrassed her that she had been a late starter, first discovering her talent at the age of nine. "I'm not one of these girls that says, 'I learned to sing right when I learned to talk – I started harmonising when I was four and a half," Katy laughed. "It's like, 'Right. See ya later! I was still on the bottle!'"

However, she soon made up for lost time, enrolling in music lessons at the Santa Barbara Christian school. It was a large group and, once again, Katy found herself struggling for the position of top dog – yet the competition only spurred her on. Tutor Nathan Kreitzer told the author, "Katy was part of a large class which just happened to be full of leaders, people who are extremely talented and are looking for attention and leadership. As a result, it was an extremely energetic and at times unruly class. Not only was Katy energetic, as most kids are at that age, but she seemed determined to be in front of the audience."

The curriculum offered plenty of opportunities to do that, with regular school musicals held in the chapel, and a tough programme of study. "Believe it or not, I had my elementary students doing rudiments of music, including note recognition, notation, rhythm, music appreciation and sight singing. In addition to that, we had two bell ensembles, three choirs and group piano classes," Nathan continued. "It was all pretty amazing for a small Christian school."

While the class was full of talented children, Katy seemed to have the edge over her peers. "I'm sure her background in the church had much to do with her singing and early interest in music," Nathan recalled. "She was already a talented vocalist when she was in my classes. She was rebellious but, to be fair, those kids who are destined to do great things tend to be agitators."

Katy formed a close bond with Nathan, who – unlike others – looked fondly on her indiscretions. While she was the "black sheep" in a family of religious pastors, she found an outlet for her rebellious behaviour in his classes. Yet while she might have been the risqué one in a religious environment, nothing could have prepared Katy for secondary school. Having attended only Christian faith schools in the past, when she was enrolled in a secular public high school, Dos Pueblos, it was to be the biggest shock of her life.

A whole new world began to open for her, but first she had to find her feet. At the start she was teased relentlessly for her squeaky clean image and tendency to moralise. Katy found her classmates' worldliness exciting, but was troubled by the division between them and her Christian friends. These were the people her parents had warned her about and yet she found herself enjoying their company. "When I faced public high school, I didn't exclude myself from the worldly kids," she recalled to *Christian Music Central*. "I just tried to be myself and show love to everybody. Not in an in-your-face, happy all the time way – just keeping it real so that I would influence my friends in love and in Christ. Sometimes I wasn't a great witness, but I think that I did make a positive impact on my peers by my actions."

While she was trying to find her feet in high school, she continued to pursue music. She would be invited to perform at the Santa Barbara Farmer's Market – just her with her voice and the battered blue guitar she had received as a 13th birthday gift from her church. "This was one way of making money as a young kid," Katy told *Philstar*. "It was fun because people would buy their fruit and vegetables and there was a violinist in one corner, there's a kid doing some kind of drum interpretation and then there was me at 13 in my own little corner, singing my own silly songs." She added, "It was a great experience. It was great to be in front of people when you want to be in the music industry because it gives you a great read."

Although the small crowds that gathered to buy farm foods didn't provide Katy with the widespread adulation she craved, it gave her a taste of the thrill of being in front of an audience – and she wanted more. However, if it hadn't been for Action House Ministry, Katy's dreams might never have gone any further.

Carol Thomas was one of the founders of Action House, a Christian organisation which worked tirelessly to keep homeless people off the street and to spread the word of God. She needed a promotions girl and felt the angelic, fresh-faced young Katy would be the perfect person. It wasn't just her image but her voice that wowed and she was soon invited on trips with Carol, accompanied by one or both of her parents. "I travelled in my motor home and she and her mom took the maiden voyage with me," Carol told the author. "Katy was so interested in music that I gave her all of my old 33⅓ records, with probably some 45s thrown in."

"Action House travelled from city to city doing outreaches in churches showing the love of Christ and using the gifts and talents of the youths," she recalled. "Katy sang 'Shine Jesus Shine' and 'When We All Get To Heaven' by Crystal Lewis. She usually sang before an altar call and made a definite impact on the crowd. She had an extremely gifted voice and range."

Katy became the vocal spokesperson for Action House wherever in the country they went. Her parents were relieved that singing was keeping their highly strung daughter occupied and out of trouble, but – most importantly – felt that her activities counterbalanced the "immorality" she might encounter at her secular school on weekdays. Meanwhile, Carol recalled that the main message was "for all to have a personal relationship with Jesus and accept the free gift of eternal life".

Being able to do something she loved to promote that message renewed Katy's faith and enthusiasm for God. She told *Cross Rhythms*: "I heard a saying that people will influence a person daily hundreds of times and that made me think, 'Wow! I could influence a person just by doing something, being aware of something or being somewhere.'"

She added: "I was one of these kids going to camp and every time there was an altar call, I was there... I grew up knowing about Christ and Christianity [but] I didn't actually make it my own until I was going through a process when I was 13. It's becoming a more personalised faith to me daily because I actually realised that my parents weren't my salvation and they weren't the ones that were going to be judged – just because they're Christians and pastors doesn't make me shiny and new. Salvation is for everyone but you have to make a personal choice."

It might have sounded as though Katy was plagued with guilt and fear, but she insisted that her commitment was her decision alone. "I came to a realisation that I'm believing because I'm believing, not because it's been thrown in my face all of these years," she claimed. "Basically I just have adopted it as my own faith and grown out of the mode of letting it be a family tradition. I know that God had been knocking on my door for quite a while and God was the only person that truly understands me completely, because I'm such an outcast and a kooky little funky person."

Katy's positive experiences singing with the ministry led to her becoming protective of the genre. She believed she'd found the style of music for her, telling *Christian Retailing*:"I think even as us in the Christian industry, we should always be pushing the envelope, trying to be something a little bit better than the mainstream is! We shouldn't be influenced by them, they should be influenced by us! The whole time we're influenced by them, we're so far behind that the average person's ear doesn't want to listen to it. I think we're worth more than that."

Maintaining that her loyalties lay firmly with gospel music, she controversially added: "Obviously [the mainstream] is not serving God, they're not in it for the same motives that we're in it for. They're in it for something totally different, whatever reason they may be in it for, and we have the ultimate Creator… we ought to be the best at what we do. Not second, but the best. God is our God!"

Yet behind the scenes, Katy longed for a fix of secular music and, one day, she let her curiosity get the better of her. The first time she succumbed to temptation, smuggling an Incubus CD into the house, it broke in half before she even got it home. Could it have been a warning from God?

"I don't know, it was just one of those moments," Katy told *SF Gate*. "Imagine being a 13-year-old kid and something like that happening. I was like, 'I'll never do it again!'"

Ghost stories had been banned altogether in Katy's house, just like at *Jesus Camp*, so the band name's reference to a spirit that preyed sexually on unsuspecting women as they slept would not have been well received by Katy's parents. But above all, it was a "lawless" secular rock band – and it was strictly forbidden.

If her family took exception to Incubus, that was nothing to how they might have felt if they had learnt that their daughter was also listening to Queen, whose frontman was known as the controversial "queen of camp", Freddie Mercury. Katy had made friends with a worldlier girl in high school who had introduced her to the classics of rock music – and it was a defining moment for her.

"I remember vividly – I was over at my friend's house and we were trying on all her clothes and it was like a scene in a movie.

She put on a CD and it was 'Killer Queen' and everything just flowed," she told *Star Pulse*. "We stopped dancing and sat on the edge of the bed listening to the lyrics of the song and thinking, 'Oh my Gosh!'"

No longer did Katy want to emulate the gospel greats of her era — she had found a new role model. "It was a moment where everything kind of went in slow motion. The clouds moved away, the sun started shining and I was like, 'I've found it! I've found an artist I want to be like!'" she enthused. "Everybody has that one person they want to be, that poster on the wall — Elvis, Madonna. For me it was 'Killer Queen' — I wanted to be like Freddie Mercury."

She later told *E! Entertainment* that her whole world had stopped, claiming, "I thought, 'I want to be like a crazy, spitfire, ballsy, killer queen who doesn't take no for an answer.'" Freddie might have been at odds with her parents' worldview, with his flamboyant clothes, the openly gay lifestyle that saw him die prematurely of AIDS and the pounding rock music that had made his career — but an infatuated Katy was prepared to take that risk.

Before long, it was her worldview that was changing. She spoke of hymns that she had previously belted out with enthusiasm by snapping that she had sung them "until I was blue in the face". She then surreptitiously introduced new artists into her musical vocabulary. "I became like a sponge, soaking up pop culture from Madonna to The Beach Boys — I was so open to experiencing new things and new ideas," she *told E! Entertainment*.

When New Kids On The Block made their comeback, Katy was hearing it for the first time around. "I didn't get to see a lot of the pop culture of the nineties," she told *Dutch ElleGirl*. "I have no idea what happened! The New Kids on the Block are still the NEW Kids on the Block to me. I can't hear anything old from it. Quite funny!"

However, it wasn't the innocent candy-coated boy bands with their stories of falling in love that attracted Katy. She was interested in "strong women" such as Fiona Apple, Gwen Stefani, Shirley Manson, Joan Jett and Cyndi Lauper. She also respected Madonna for being older yet relevant and "cool as fuck".

One of her ultimate favourites however was Alanis Morissette. "The *Jagged Little Pill* record was a big influence on me," she told *Star Pulse*. "Everybody listened to that record and there was a song, if not all of them, that related to everyone. It was a soundtrack to life. I would listen to it for the summer over and over."

Katy was inspired by these artists and set about practising guitar every spare moment of the day, until her "fingertips bled". Her biggest role model was Freddie Mercury – another artist who lacked self-consciousness. To Katy, whose every move was scrutinised by her family to keep her behaviour pure and Christian, his total lack of censorship was deeply inspiring. "Freddie Mercury was a bad ass," she laughed to *BBC Entertainment*. "It was kinda like he didn't care what anybody thought about him – he always brought the entertainment value to the show."

Referring to Queen's controversial hit 'Fat Bottomed Girls', she said, "Who would have thought that you would write a song about girls with big asses? Everybody would sing along to it and, I don't know, he seemed like he had a good sense of humour in his life and was smart and intelligent and, basically, said exactly what was on his mind – and I respect that. He never censored himself for the sake of anybody." Liberation and humour were, in Katy's eyes, sorely lacking in her household. Yet she still loved her parents and respected their faith.

In fact, referring to her parents' antics in their earlier years, she insisted, "They're a different breed of Christians... sometimes people envisage my parents wearing the priest outfit and I'm like, 'No, actually, my dad has four tattoos.' I mean, they all happen to say Jesus, but he's kind of like a modern rock 'n' roll pastor himself. We definitely agree to disagree on some things but I don't think that's unusual for a kid and their parents' relationship."

While her father was not a conventional preacher, her tastes in music were still not approved of. Listening to household names in music with whom most children had grown up became a coveted privilege that Katy would have to beg for. "I started little by little, asking, 'Hey, you know, can I listen to The Beatles?'" she told *CBS News*. "And I had friends that influenced their taste on me. You know, friends that

I looked up to that were so much cooler – they knew about the world, you know? And I was just, 'Wow, teach me everything!'"

At around the same time, Katy took up dancing, yet another forbidden fruit in the eyes of her family. "I would go to the Santa Barbara Recreational Hall and I would learn how to dance there," she told *Artist Direct*. "I was taught by some of the more seasoned dancers who were actually very involved in the scene. These girls would get out of their old vintage Cadillacs with their pencil skirts and their tight little cardigans and I thought it was so unique and different to what was going on in the 2000s... I was really attracted to having my own sense of style because I started swing dancing, lindy hop and jitterbug."

The fascination she felt for these sexually powerful veteran dancers who seemed to have their look arranged to a T prompted Katy to reinvent her own style. "The forties have always been my biggest inspiration because I loved the way that the women held themselves," she told *Black Book*. "Everything was very manicured. Sure, they had pencil skirts on and big sweaters, but underneath that pencil skirt and that sweater, you know, that girl had a bullet bra, garter and stockings. She knew she was so sexy, and she didn't have to tell anybody and that was, I think, so cool."

This metaphor seems perfect for Katy's early life. She was outwardly God-fearing and respectable, but underneath her mask was a girl who totally contradicted that image and was yearning to break free; a girl who'd sing along to Queen's 'Fat Bottomed Girls' as loudly as the next person and who didn't hide her sexuality for a moment.

Katy also enjoyed the Betty Boop brand of sexuality, claiming, "I'm very into the Varga girls and the pin-up girls and those girls who are almost accidentally in trouble because the dog leash got wrapped around their skirt and you can see a pink bow flashing outside their garters."

She was a secret fan of Courtney Love's baby-doll dresses with sweetheart necklines, too. Courtney's outrageous, trashy but girlish look had even given birth to a style known as kinder-whore. It was characterised by leopard print, pastel pinks, glitter, Powerpuff Girl tees and brightly coloured children's jewellery.

On one rare occasion, she had been allowed to actually buy one of the fashion items she craved – but it backfired. "I had the coolest fake leopard-print coat – I went to school wearing this coat [but] everyone made fun of me," a crestfallen Katy recalled to *The Guardian*. "I sold it to the secondhand clothes shop two years later to get more clothes."

Another fashion model for Katy was Lolita, the teenage temptress in the Vladimir Nabokov novel of the same name. This desire to emulate Lolita seemed symbolic of the conflict between the sexually attractive young woman she aspired to be and the innocent God-fearing youngster her parents might have preferred to raise. The Lolita look allowed Katy to be innocent yet provocative, to look sexy while playing safe under the guise of an unassuming, wholesome young girl. Katy claimed that while she'd had to grow up fast, she "wanted to be a child forever".

Yet Katy couldn't hide behind the curtain of childhood for much longer. As she grew up, she had to face the ultimate taboo in a preacher's family – a lesbian crush. She told the German magazine *Bravo*, "When I fell in love for the first time, I didn't fall in love with a boy – her name was Anna! We shared everything, as best friends do. Anna was incredibly pretty, a sweet ballerina – she was perfect. Unfortunately we never kissed each other – what a shame!"

Homosexuality was strictly forbidden in the Bible, so Katy had to deny her feelings and, like many of the new feelings that troubled her, she kept it quiet. She tried to repress her style leanings too. In spite of her flamboyant fashion fantasies – including a lime green polka dot skirt with a pink satin lining that she'd brought from a Betsy Johnson store – in reality, she played it safe, dressing down in jeans and T-shirts.

While she listened to secular music in secret, her public face to the world was still pure religion. She claimed that the world was crying out for bands that spoke about God, telling *Cross Rhythms*: "I think a lot of people my age, we're looking for something real. I think everyone's tired of everyone slapping a bow on Christianity and saying, 'This is actually just about Jesus' – and they whisper it. They don't want any of that any more, they want somebody to step in their face and say, 'Hey, what's up, don't be stupid – Jesus Christ is the only way.'" She added:

"I've grown up knowing that God gives this great gift called salvation which we all need because we can't breathe on our own. We need hope in our lives and God is basically it."

Katy had decided she wanted God to "take control" of her life, but – as an adult – would she continue to follow that path, or would she start to take responsibility for choosing her own? With such conflicts lying ahead of her, perhaps it was little wonder that Katy was in no hurry to grow up.

Chapter 2

A Clean Cut Christina

During this turbulent period of Katy's life, the one thing that remained consistent was her love of music. Nevertheless, for a girl who wanted to be a killer queen, her parents' prying eyes guaranteed it would be no easy road to follow.

"Katy once joked that her family were like security staff at an airport," an anonymous school friend revealed. "There was a big list of items that wouldn't get past the censors – only instead of sharp objects, it was things like CDs of Madonna! Her family probably saw her as a heathen. It was like that for most of us at our school, but Katy's parents were probably particularly strict."

She needed to find a way to combine these two major parts of her life – and she succeeded when she recorded a demo at a music-friendly Christian organisation called The Dream Center. Once there, she found that her parents weren't the only ones who believed in her. Music producer David Henley saw potential in her too. According to him, "She had the platform to change the world."

He told the author, "I knew the first time I met Katy that she was destined for greatness. Katy and my daughter were youth camp friends and she was a big part of worship at our church. She had the life and energy unlike anyone I had ever met." He continued: "I produced a demo for her in our studio that was mainly for the Christian market but had great crossover appeal. Katy was blessed by God with so many talents."

His words inspired her but, despite his encouragement, she had little imagined what was to come. Her demo, merely a casual jamming session to channel Katy's creative energy during a period of boredom, had come to the attention of Dr Pamplin, the head of both an evangelical church and a Christian music label, Red Hill Records, based in Nashville, Tennessee, the home of country music. It was perfect timing. Red Hill had been scouting for a new artist – someone as attention-grabbing as Christina Aguilera and Britney Spears but with a more clean-cut image. They sought someone with the edginess of a mainstream pop act but who could be marketed in a Christian-friendly format – and that person was Katy.

An anonymous label employee revealed: "We were looking for an artist who could hold the public's attention just as keenly as Christina [later did] in her 'Dirrrty' video, writhing around a boxing ring in little more than leather chaps – but for all the right reasons. Someone who could be a positive role model. We needed someone who could promote the message of God just as powerfully." Could Katy be the angelic pop princess that the label craved?

However Katy, a true California girl at heart, already had serious reservations. She told *Christian Contemporary Music*: "In Santa Barbara I'm five minutes from the beach, ten minutes from the mountains – I'm never moving to Nashville!"

This would be just the first in a series of increasingly outspoken confessions. Katy refused to conform to the role of a God-fearing female artist from the start, instead embarking on a path of reckless honesty. According to some onlookers, it was a move that would spell career suicide. She might have had the support of parentally approved veterans in the Christian music industry, but Katy's career looked ill-fated from the start.

Despite that, her parents believed she had what it took to succeed in the gospel industry and approved her trip to Nashville with their blessings. However, far from the risqué glamour queen that she would later become, Katy was at that time awkward, shy and totally unaccustomed to performing outside of churches or youth groups.

Fortunately she had a friend who could help out. "My other family back then was this hippie surfer family whose kids I knew from my Christian school," Katy told *Christian Music Central*. "I would haul my guitar over there and they would teach me chords here and there, and worship songs, which is where I borrowed most of the chords for my record."

Armed with the battered blue guitar that had been her most treasured possession in her teenage years, Katy also sought the help of local guitar coach Agatha Carubia. Each week she would take a one-hour private lesson at Santa Barbara's Music Academy of the West. "I encouraged her because she was not only talented, but she was living her artistry already," Agatha told the author. "She was intense and single-minded, decisive and strong. Katy was a teenager with a plan."

With time to spare before her trip to Nashville, Katy took advice from Agatha on both guitar playing and vocal training, keenly practising her songwriting skills between visits. Agatha explained: "In the lessons we worked on classical vocal technique to exercise the full range of the voice. Our emphasis was on her breathing and understanding the acoustical shift in her middle voice. I made sure she knew how to warm up. Katy enjoyed the technical aspect we worked on because it gave her ease in her songs and consistency with her whole voice. She learned how to take care of her voice – she wanted [success] very seriously."

Agatha was impressed by Katy's ease with her guitar. "She would take it out in the most natural fashion and play it in a fluid way. She and her guitar were close."

However it was her single-minded attitude that struck her tutor the most. Despite her inexperience, the sessions had helped the young singer to build an identity. "Katy completely knew who she was as an artist. She wrote her own songs," Agatha recalled. "This was more important than anything else." Katy concurred, later telling *Christian Retailing*, "I really do respect singer-songwriters because it's an original. It's not a copy! It comes straight from your heart."

It was to continue working on these songs that Katy finally booked herself on an aeroplane to Nashville, where she would learn her craft with the help of experienced producers and writers. Tennessee was notorious for its religious connections, boasting a large Christian music contingent, although the state had also borne a wave of more rebellious artists such as Kings of Leon and – to a lesser extent – Justin Timberlake. Katy was thrilled at the thought of joining their ranks but, in spite of that, there was an undertone that Nashville was not where she wanted to be. "My parents started realising that their connections were just straight to Nashville and, being as young as I was, there were no ifs, ands or buts about it all," she told *Star Pulse*.

Nevertheless, her new mentors taught Katy everything she needed to know. "So I'd go to Nashville and I'd be around all these veteran music writers and they would show me how to carve a song," she recalled. "I saw how important that was and it just gave me a format. You need to have an arch in the middle [of each song]. You want to have your verse, chorus, verse, chorus, bridge and then chorus. I didn't know that – it can be so many different ways and you don't even have to have rules to writing a song."

By this point, Katy had just turned 16 but her love of songwriting meant her education had to take a back seat. She enrolled herself in a home-schooling programme on the Internet, telling *Christian Retailing*: "I really wish I could go to high school. I went there for a semester and I loved it. [But] you have to sacrifice some things. Everyone's thinking, 'Oh, she has to sacrifice working and school – pity, pity, pity! I'm going to cry a little river for you!' It's just that I always want to keep my brain on and keep learning."

When Katy started out in Nashville, she was extremely nervous. "It seemed like everybody knew everybody else and I didn't know anyone. It made me feel like the new kid all over again, just like growing up," she told *Christian Music Central*. "I would even feel intimidated about playing the five chords I know pretty well."

However, she needn't have worried. She had a willing mentor in the form of co-writer Brian White – and he saw past her nerves instantly. "When Katy walked into the publishing company to write, I immediately knew she had the IT factor," he told the author. "And it wasn't some over the top 'I wanna be a star' attitude – just a teenage girl with a love for music and an unbelievable amount of talent and drive and a faith that she was not ashamed of. It was like lightning in a bottle, and you knew once you took the lid off, it was gonna be amazing."

He also channelled her creativity. "At the time that I worked with Katy, she was a teenager and the world was a playground to her," he recalled. "Being in Nashville was a different experience and I wanted her to not get overwhelmed with this new freedom and to stay grounded and focused on what we were doing. Let's face it, music is fun, should be fun and it was fun. But there is a serious side to making a record. It is a piece of you and you are giving it to the rest of the world. Words, once said are hard to get back. You either live them or eat them. I didn't want to be her parents because she already had them – and what amazing people they are – but I wanted to be that friend and voice of reason to help guide her in this first time experience."

At Brian's request, Katy wrote devotionals for every song – short themed essays featuring the Biblical references that summed up the inspiration for each one. Ensuring that Katy expressed a Christian message that would reach out to others like her and fit in with the vision of the record company was his main goal. "Working on a Christian record, of course the focus is the message and making sure it is all theologically sound," he recalled. "Katy really wanted to challenge her audience as well as share her struggles in a very transparent way. Truth was important and her honesty was amazing. For me, working with a raw, open book made for songs that went straight to the heart. Katy was not ashamed to talk about her faith and knew this was the calling of her life."

He added of the devotionals: "They were kind of like a Bible study that the listener could use while listening to the project. It was to be a glimpse into where these songs came from and why she felt compelled to write them, with the scripture references that fit the message of the song. It was my way to try and get a multiaged audience to listen to a teenager and her art and take her seriously – to know this was more than music, it was the heart and soul of someone who was passionate about her faith."

According to Philip Von Wrede, the label's marketing and sales coordinator, Katy had desperately needed that mentoring. "I felt that stage of Katy's life was her teenage frumpy stage and that she still needed to get comfortable in her skin. Dino, the boss, was helping sculpt her to modernise her sound from the traditional Christian contemporary sound that she was used to singing in churches. Katy, in the beginning, came over a little shy. The overall experience was overwhelming for her, going to a new level. I think Katy was listening to a lot of people and trying to please everyone."

Indeed, Katy admitted this herself, telling *Christian Retailing* of making the album, "Too many influences on you, you don't know what to do. Everyone was like, 'Be that way' and I was like, 'God, just help me to know what I want to be!' Sure, you can always sit and listen to what people have to say, but most of it's bad for your ear."

Katy was a curious mixture of cockiness and insecurity – and she knew she was having an identity crisis. Her aim was to strike a balance between cooperating with others and saying what she wanted to say. In the very first song that she wrote, Katy was able to achieve this. When she penned 'Trust In Me', she had been succumbing to self-doubt, wondering whether she really deserved the opportunity the record label had given her. The song referred candidly to the gulf between who she was and who she believed others wanted her to be.

In fact, behind the scenes, Katy was going through major conflict. "When I first got signed, I was at a place in my life where I was like, 'I don't know if I can hold that promise [to wait until marriage] because this guy at camp is really cute.' Sex wasn't talked about in my home, except for the basics," she told *Effect Radio*.

'Trust In Me' addressed the guilt she felt at whether she was pleasing her parents, her record label and of course God, while still being true to herself. "Even with this tremendous blessing and opportunity of making a record, I still focused on my faults and wondered if I was acceptable to God," she told *Christian Music Central* of the song. "I was just dealing with the fact that I could still be loved. That's an aspect of grace that I may not ever understand."

She added on her personal website: "I was feeling a little depressed at the time and was thinking about all the things I'd done wrong. I felt like I was oil and God was water and I just wouldn't mix. I started writing about this and God placed a peace in my heart. I really felt he was saying,

'Don't worry, child, trust in me.' I just had to open my heart to the healing process."

Talking of the conflict Katy felt between her private self and her professional self, Philip Von Wrede told the author: "I think for so long she sang about what she thought people wanted to hear rather than what she felt. To her, being that she felt anti-Nashville, I believe the mainstream market was closer to where she really wanted to go. She really didn't like the idea that all Christian artists move to Nashville. I believe she felt more at home in California and with the mentality of Californians. She was a little grungy, wearing baggier clothes and little make-up, and in my opinion was still trying to find her style and look."

He added: "As she got more comfortable in her own skin, she realised the Christian market may not have been open to the views or thoughts she felt. Back then, on a professional level, she stayed religious. However, personally she probably displayed to her close friends her wild side and her real views on issues."

She was struggling with the choices that being an adult offered, balancing temptation with a desire to please. Aptly then, another track on the album was titled 'Growing Pains'. Katy saw the song as a slightly aggressive anthem for misunderstood teenagers who were persecuted for their age. "Kids don't like being written off as if they didn't know much about God or what they really believe in," Katy wrote on her website. "Sometimes older people can stereotype this generation because of what they've been told – basically the lies that say we aren't any good, or all we do is drugs and get into a bunch of trouble. It's not true. I haven't ever seen an age limit on who God can use." Unusually, the earnest gospel-themed message combined itself with an alternative rock melody that could easily have been inspired by Queen's 'Bohemian Rhapsody'.

From the beginning Katy had never been a conventional Christian writer and 'Piercing' was another song with a twist. "The heart and soul of the song came from Katy," co-writer Brian White told the author. "She wanted a song that made a statement about her commitment. The word 'piercing' was perfect for how she felt the Lord was cutting deep into her soul, a strong and visual word to bring the passion of her love for Christ out in a song."

At first it seemed to be yet another innocent ode to God's word, but after a night performing at Brian's local church youth group, the title took on a whole new meaning. "It was just Katy and her acoustic guitar," he recalled. "Besides being a major talent, she has a huge personality so the youth at my church immediately fell in love with her. Later that night, we went back to my house, ordered pizza and just hung out listening to music and talking with my kids. My son Blair, a guitar player and writer himself, loved what she did musically, not to mention he found her easy to look at."

However, it was with Brian's daughter that Katy's truly mischievous side came into play. "Katy and my daughter Brooke hit it off on the fashion front and Brooke loved that Katy had her nose pierced. A little while later, the two of them disappeared and, the next thing I knew, we found them in the bathroom with an ice-cube and a needle and Katy was piercing my daughter's nose! We still laugh about that story to this day and I found it particularly amusing that we had just written a song called 'Piercing' together for Katy's record — how appropriate!"

Katy's love of God also emerged in songs such as 'When There's Nothing Left', which described an unconventional relationship with her creator. Competitive as ever, she had wanted to outdo writers of traditional love songs and create one with a twist — one that depicted a romance not with a boyfriend or a husband, but with God.

She wrote on her website: "This song is a crisp, clean, simple 'love note' to God. I was thinking of how many instances we have these love stories about couples doing whatever they have to do to be together — they would even die to be together. I wanted to write about a more famous love story — one that did do everything so that we could be together eternally. I wrote as though I was in love romantically with Him, like I would always give Him all of me even when I didn't have any more to give."

Mainstream Christians failed to appreciate the sentiments, leaving some open-mouthed. "This is what I would call blasphemy," complained one anonymous blogger. "She should think more carefully before she speaks."

She raised eyebrows again with 'Last Call', a song inspired by a book she had been reading, *Last Call For Help* by Dawson McAllister. Dawson was a Christian talk-show host and agony uncle who had been inspired to write about his experiences talking desperate teenagers out of self-harm, suicide and violence. In the song, Katy urged teenagers to turn to God with that cry for help, substituting the telephone number of Dawson's helpline with that of her father's church.

While she was adding the finishing touches to the song, her father stepped into the picture. Not realising she had been reading the book, he claimed to have had a prophetic vision suggesting that she write a song about a last call for help. That was all Katy needed to know – and another song was born. She recalled on her website: "I made the character realise that this phone call to God for help was the best one he ever made."

Katy demonstrated the intensity of her beliefs again in 'Faith Won't Fail'. The song depicted her throwing caution to the winds and surrendering to blind faith and was littered with Biblical references to salvation, where faith had prevailed. She recounted the story of Daniel, who had been flung into a den of lions, but had survived when God, realising his innocence, had sent an angel to close their jaws and fend off their urge for human blood. She also name-checked the story of Peter, who was able to walk on water to reach Jesus' outstretched hands. The moment he looked away from his saviour, he had begun to sink into the ocean but – provided he kept his eyes and focus on Jesus – he escaped from drowning. This was exactly the type of blind faith Katy wanted to bring to life in the song.

"They had the faith to look past their problems," she enthused on her website. "A lot of times I'll get distracted and lose focus in my relationship with Christ. I try to keep on and have that persistent faith to get me through things and even that small little mustard seed of faith always moves my mountains." Yet there were still times when Katy was fearful and unsure of herself. Despite her determination, the album also had a dark side. For example, at early shows with church youth groups, Katy had jokingly asked the audience if they shared her teenage insecurities and still slept with nightlights. Met with deafening roars of approval, she realised she needed to write a song that reached out to those who felt the same. Titled 'My Own Monster', she hoped that it would inspire them to combat fear.

"I exposed one of my more personal secrets," Katy explained on the website, "that I too struggle with fear. One night I realised I needed God to help me, to hold me, as the chorus says. Growing up, my parents would tell me to pray when I got scared and tell the devil to flee. I remembered all that and wanted to write about how I find my refuge underneath His wings. You can't open up to fear – it'll eat you up."

She added to *Christian Music Central* of the song: "It's really just about your worst enemy being yourself. When you allow fear into your spirit, you give the enemy an open door to your mind and your heart."

Why had Katy been fearful? Living in a strict Christian household, she struggled under the weight of her family's expectations and was torn between following her parents' wishes and following her heart. In fact, it was Katy's mother who had named her next tune.

'Spit', a song about infidelity to God, acted out some of her guilt at living a "life of sin". Although she directed it at "hypocritical", supposedly clean-living Christian classmates, could the song also have been autobiographical?

She claimed on her website: "I was wondering how people would change and shape up if Christ was here attending my school. I was like, if Jesus came back as a simple high school kid, how would you act in front of Him? Don't you understand the pain He feels when you do these things – basically, spit in his face? It's a mockery. But there's the truth."

She added, "When you ask Christ into your heart, He's there in your heart, wherever you go. He sees it all. I want people to understand that it hurts Christ when they ignore him and live their lives. The pain is like crucifying Him again and again. But can you believe it? He forgives everything."

However, it was 'Search Me' that offered the most insight into her conflicts, asking God why she hides behind a mask and plays hide and seek when she knows He can tell exactly what is on her mind and what lies behind her exterior.

Meanwhile, 'Naturally' was a prophetic song that seemed to foretell Katy's future. It spoke of living alone, succumbing to a loss of control and not finding the answers she would like to hear. Just a few years later, Katy would embark on a similar lonely journey as she was rejected by record labels, living away from home. She would turn away from God as the song described and instead party her way to mainstream success. Just 15 when she composed the tune, Katy had little idea of what was ahead of her, but the song ended on a positive note, depicting salvation.

"I believe some teens have their loneliest moments during this time of their lives," she claimed on her website. "I think they are going through the trials of growing up and all that comes with it, whether it be issues with parents or thinking that they are the only ones going through what they are going through. They don't realise that they have a best friend that has never let them down – someone that is on their side. He understands it all." She was, of course, referring to God.

As Katy struggled to find the confidence she needed to mould her stage persona, it was again God that she turned to – in fact, she believed that He was the only one who truly knew who she was. Depicting her creator as someone who knew her better than she did, she appealed to Him for help as her dreams of being on the stage finally came true.

She recalled on her website, "I was struggling with the fact that I would have the huge responsibility of how others would be affected through what I was saying or doing on stage. I don't want to put on some kind of front that everything is good when it's not. I wanted to keep it real but still give people hope. I was trying to figure out how to combine the two, so I put my gifts on the shelf for a period of time."

She continued, "I looked back and realised that God was with me through this season of my life. He knew one day I would wake up and remember the amazing gift I was given and how so many other people would love to be on the stage that I had been letting collect dust."

However, for Katy that was all about to change. Her album was complete and, far from collecting dust, she was ready to win over new audiences. By now, she had broken the promise she'd made to herself never to live in Nashville, moving in with her publicist, Mandy Collinger-Parsons, instead. She put down roots in the city, dating a local boy and making a firm friendship with Mandy.

Speaking about the period, Mandy told the author: "Katy is so loving and caring. In one instance, I left work early to go pick her up for her boyfriend's school Battle of the Bands competition. I got into a major car accident on the way over and when she found out, she rushed to the hospital. She felt like it was all her fault and was by my side the entire time."

However, much of Katy's time in Nashville ran smoothly and Red Hill was delighted with her album. The next step was to find her a manager. Fortunately for her, she already had a company willing to sign her – Christian rock artist Jennifer Knapp and her business partner Steven Thomas had set up Alabaster Arts in a bid to discover rock talent and Katy had impressed them from the moment they saw her at a casual California in-store appearance.

"We waited for years to find the right artist," Steven recalled. "Katy had the right combination of talent and heart. We hesitated to sign a teenager, but Katy pulled us by our heartstrings from the very beginning. We believe that she has staying power, primarily because she's a strong songwriter."

Jennifer was equally concerned about signing Katy at the tender age of 16. "We had a really hard time going, 'I don't know if I want to get into this.' I don't agree, for lack of a better term, with pimping an artist to sell records," she explained. However, after some soul-searching and a little persuasion from Katy's eager parents, the two came to a mutual decision.

"The issue was whether we were going to invest there and then and take the ridicule of having signed a young artist, or allow her to take some other avenue without someone who cares for her," Jennifer recalled of the signing. "It sounds egotistical to think we'd be able to do that, but I would consider us failures if we didn't do that for her. We're not set up to make money... we want her parents to call the shots. We're really not trying to take over the world with her. I think that's a couple of years off – I'd like her to be able to vote first!"

Katy might have been young, but she was already making waves. Her debut concert for a songwriters' night at the Douglas Corner Cafe in Nashville saw her intimidating seasoned veterans three times her age. At that time, Katy's look was diminutive and unassuming – she wore little make-up and had not yet developed a strong stage presence or sense of style. Yet, according to onlookers, the crowd's indifference was transformed the moment she started singing. On hearing her song 'Search Me', a fellow songwriter exclaimed: "That just makes me mad! How old are you again? That's not fair." It was the acclaim that Katy had longed for.

With a manager in tow, it was now time to take her show on the road. Katy's quirky, unconventional edge quickly proved a burden for her, but fortunately like-minded people were on the touring circuit with her who could cushion her fall. In February 2001, she embarked on a nationwide tour with the Christian performers V*enna, Earthsuit and Phil Joel.

Katy and Adam LaClave, the lead singer of fellow support group Earthsuit, bonded quickly. They were both outsiders in Christian culture – Adam for fronting a punk rock band and Katy for simply being herself. "The Christian market absolutely didn't get Katy," Adam told the author. "Her music fit the bill perfectly but her personality on and offstage was way too uncontrollable for the powers that be. In Christian contemporary music, the music you make is actually just a small factor in your success. Your willingness to play the game and project yourself well as a role model to the sub-culture is really the biggest component to getting the Jesusbux." *

Despite her best intentions, Katy was far from a role model. Adam revealed: "Katy would burp on stage and wore tight shirts showing off her big perfectly shaped breasts, so yeah, I guess you could say she was doomed in a way from the start while in the Christian market."

Both Adam and Katy were on a tour that made them feel like square pegs in round holes and they formed a close friendship on account of their isolation. "Earthsuit was on the road with her and a handful of other bands and we were kind of an odd band to be on that tour, with the mostly adult contemporary pop-rock kind of stuff that filled the rest of the bill," Adam recalled. "I got really bored with the tone of that tour and the crowds were mostly a bore, so hanging out and joking around with Katy was really the only element of fun that I can remember."

---

* Income derived from Christian music.

He continued: "She kind of became like a younger sister in a way and would do anything that she thought might get a laugh. I remember one time all the bands were doing a meet and greet where the fans come through a long line of autographs and pictures and I suggested that instead of signing anything that she take the sharpie and just write all over herself. Well, without hesitation, she started screaming and laughing and just covering her entire face with black marker. I'm pretty sure she scarred some Christian music-loving kids that day – you know, the ones who masturbate to her videos while praying for her to return to God."

Fellow Christians both shuddered and smiled as she met with fans with "I'm Katy" emblazoned across her forehead and hastily smudged black marker around her eyes. Totally unafraid of her imperfections, she had highlighted a spot on her chin by drawing a star around it and had even blackened out one of her teeth.

Her other misadventures included making a beeline for every policeman she saw, flirting and curtsying and asking to play with his gun. On another occasion, she became so excited while telling a story in a Nashville restaurant that she sent several chairs flying across the room.

Full of youthful exuberance and thrilled to be on the road for the first time, Katy ensured there was never a dull moment. She was determined that the world should be her playground.

Yet some took a dimmer view of her antics. "Katy was happy to make a fool of herself for attention," an anonymous member of her tour crew claimed. "It was eye-wateringly embarrassing, especially for some of the more conservative Christians among us. She would do interviews and start flirting with guys almost three times her age. She'd be this young teenager and guys in their forties would have to guiltily back away from her."

Katy was confident, flirtatious and assertive – and she quickly found the Christian outlet for her music restrictive. Everything she did seemed to be met with tuts of disapproval. Matthew Turner, the editor of *Christian Contemporary Music* magazine, interviewed Katy over that period. He told the author: "She talked about her faith a good deal, but it was often about the things that annoyed her – the rules, the limitations, the role of being a girl."

He confirmed: "I don't think Christian media was ready for a 16-year-old who spoke her mind and had a personality. At the time, most young artists in music were quiet and shy and Katy broke the mould completely."

It was equally difficult for people to put Katy's onstage persona into a category. A blogger for *Epinions* claimed of her short three-song set: "We weren't sure whether to expect lay-your-soul-bare folk tunes or bubblegum pop, since it was just Katy and her guitar." To their surprise, they got neither – but a light rock sound that was entirely her own.

The review continued: "They were a memorable three songs, perfectly displaying her budding songwriting skills and her impressive vocals. Throughout the concert, we kept leaning over and whispering to each other that we detected another influence in her vocal style. Jewel, Sarah McLachlan, Christina Aguilera and once again, the inescapable comparisons to Jennifer Knapp. Her ballad 'Search Me' would have been right at home on an album by the Kansas folkster, although her charming between-song banter with the audience gave away her Los Angeles valley girl roots. I think this girl will go far, because when all of the production is stripped away and it's just her and her guitar, she can please a crowd who's never heard of her before." Ironically, the tour had been named Strangely Normal – yet Katy was anything but.

She had also been invited to a show with Jennifer Knapp at the Glasshouse in Pamona, California, where she would be both her support act and her runner. From the beginning of the evening, Katy had stuck out like a sore thumb. Playing to a devout and conservative Christian crowd, she had taken to the stage in short, bright red hot pants.

"When you saw me, you knew it was me up there," Katy boasted to *The Inland Valley Daily Bulletin* of her new-found sexy look. Yet this crowd were less impressed – and disaster struck for the second time that night when a nervous Katy handed Jennifer the wrong guitar during her set, smashing it on the floor in the process.

Jennifer kindly spared Katy's blushes, recalling: "Touring is one of the hardest things a musician can do and you suffer burnout so easily. But Katy was always up for anything and she didn't complain. She knew that anyone else her age would want to be in her place. After that thing with the guitar, I could tell she was really embarrassed, so I decided to give it to her to remember that night."

She added: "No matter how big you get – and she could sing – you're not invincible, so don't take yourself too seriously. I shouldn't have bothered – Katy never needs too much help with that."

An anonymous school friend concurred: "Katy was never self-obsessed or worried about imperfections. She was kooky, a bit of a clown and didn't care. That confidence was enviable. It was the antithesis of the skinny, surgically enhanced California girl – someone who knew that her family loved her, God loved her and anyone who wasn't happy with her just the way she was could go to hell."

Although Katy appeared self-assured, she too had her moments of agonising self-doubt and uncertainty. There were times when she wondered whether a career on the stage was the right move for a good Christian girl. "I ask myself, 'Do you think Satan is going to let you twirl around like a pretty ballerina?'" she confessed to *Christian Contemporary Music*. "I really appreciate people who can slam me, who have the guts to say, 'That's not what you're supposed to be doing.'"

In that case, Katy had a long list of disapproving people to appreciate. Yet she was honest about these moments and portrayed them in songs such as 'Trust In Me'. In doing so, she hoped she could be the friend fellow teenagers had never met, voicing the confusion they shared with her about growing up and providing a source of comfort.

Above all, she wanted the album to reflect who she was. "I started writing songs when I realised that singing other people's lyrics was more an expression of their heart than mine," she told *Christian Music Central*. "Writing this album was very important to me. I felt I'd been given a message and was supposed to voice it in my own words. I want to be an artist, not just someone who puts her voice on a CD – and I didn't want to be written off as just another teenager with a record deal."

She added, "My ultimate goal is to show people that they aren't alone. If they feel they've been let down by parents, teachers, spouses or friends, there is a best friend who will never let them down." That friend was music.

She got the opportunity to communicate that message when her album debuted. Her publicist had been busy sending sample singles out with 'Search Me' and 'Last Call' on them and had recovered mainly positive responses. Then, in March 2001, the moment arrived that Katy had been waiting for – her album was finally released.

Russ Breimeier, a journalist for *Christianity Today*, one of the first to review it, enthused: "Katy Hudson's game is alternative pop/rock, much like the electronica meets folk rock sound of Fiona Apple. Her strong, throaty and sometimes soulful vocals give her a unique sound. Her songwriting style is so strong, it's difficult to believe she's only 16 – and was merely 15 when she wrote most of the songs. The lead single 'Trust In Me' features haunting strings with lots of electronica effects and solid rock roots. It's the first song she wrote and it's as good as most of what you hear on the radio!"

Praising her "dark, questioning" verses, and suggesting that the songs she wrote by herself surpassed the ones that were co-written, he added: "The lounge jazz meets art-rock feel of it is pure ear candy with the message that we're being moulded perpetually in God's image... Katy Hudson's debut easily could have been just another teen songwriter mimicking mainstream music trends with Christian lyrics. Instead I hear a remarkable young talent emerging, a gifted songwriter in her own right who will almost certainly go far in this business. That name again is Katy Hudson. Trust me, you'll be hearing more and more of it in the next year."

Katy was delighted to read the review, commenting on *Effect Radio*: "*Christianity Today* compared me to Fiona Apple and Sarah McLachlan. I thought, 'Even if this is the only album I make, I'll remember that!'"

Yet there were some who still misunderstood Katy. *AllMusic* claimed, "Perry already betrays a heavy debt to Alanis Morissette, hauling out caterwauls whenever she can. This helps give her rolling mid-tempo expressions of faith a touch of inappropriate angst." Of the song 'Growing Pains', the website commented: "Even here you can hear Perry straining against her constraints – her line, 'While the man upstairs does his work on me' is as sexually charged as anything."

Those who had heard her gush that 'When There's Nothing Left' was about a romantic love affair with God might have made the same connection, but for Katy the comparison was deeply humiliating. The review also added: "This isn't the only time there are weird carnal overtones here – there's a creeping S&M undercurrent on 'Faith Won't Fail' – she can be thrown in a cell, shackled up on the rails and still her 'faith won't fail' – that's oddly disquieting."

Even more embarrassing for Katy, after the initial flurry of reviews, there was a deathly silence. She then received some bad news – Red Hill Records would be dropping some of its artists due to financial issues. "They told me some of the female artists were going on the chopping block," Katy recalled to *Effect Radio*. "I was only 17 and I was devastated. I prayed, which I didn't do that much... Then I got an invitation to sing at [pastor and record label owner] Dr Pamplin's church because someone had given him my album and reminded him I already worked for him. I guess you could call it a miracle – but I say it's just God looking after his own."

It seemed as though Katy's faith had saved her again. Dr Pamplin was keen to hear her sing and she obliged, getting on the next flight to Oregon. "It was a pretty big crowd," she continued, "and I had a great time... when Dr Pamplin saw how much the people my age enjoyed it, I was able to stay on, even though my stuff was more pop than pure gospel."

Katy also believed she'd finally found her genre – after much experimentation with sounds inspired by everyone from Fiona Apple to Ella Fitzgerald, she decided on "folk acoustic" to be her trademark.

Despite Katy's awkwardness and the embarrassment of the faux pas dropping Jennifer Knapp's guitar, she was quickly making a name for herself as a credible live artist. Matthew Turner told the author: "While I certainly recognised that Katy had an amazing voice and good songwriting skills, it wasn't until I saw her sing live that I truly grasped the depth of her talent." He caught her opening for a Christian artist known as Bebo Norman and enthused: "The power and control of her voice was chill-inducing. Katy had sparks even at 16. She was amazing, well beyond her years and she belted out tunes with passion."

The show that had appealed to Matthew was one of a series in September and October 2001, where Katy had supported Bebo in performances at churches all around the country. Yet while Katy's voice impressed, her look in those days was nothing to write home about. It was indicative of her confusion and ongoing identity crisis – was she a woman of God or did she dare to break out from behind her demure stereotype? Though she dreamed of pin-ups and glamour girls, wanting to look like one herself, and had been buying from Betsey Johnson's fashion lines since the age of 12, at her Christian shows she found herself hiding behind tomboyish casual clothes – outfits which she saw as a safe bet.

Katy would wear baggy jeans, trainers and flip-flops and bandana-style headbands. Other concert goers described her as "a little unkempt". She had little to liven up her outfits aside from a hint of gaudy, glittery blue eyeshadow – her trademark in those days. However, according to the blog *Hail Of A Day*, what she lacked in stage presence and presentation she compensated for with "a voice that could knock down a brick wall – powerful and very controlled".

She might have seemed unremarkable at the start, but her distinctive voice and even her cheap bare-wood acoustic guitar turned out to be her secret weapons. Katy was not to be underestimated.

Even her studio recording was proving popular in the media. Russ Breimeier of *Christian Music Today* insisted: "That album made our best albums list that year. Katy had a very creative sound for Christian music, more outside the box and I thought there was a lot of potential for her to develop into something more." However, even though those in the know were warming to her album, it hadn't yet reached the majority of Christian listeners. The record company's marketing budget was small and, according to journalist DeWayne Hamby, "As an insider I heard it but I think it never really made it to the average gospel listener."

Katy's battle wasn't over and her growth as an artist was dramatically stunted when Red Hill Records went into liquidation. After months of struggle, the company had gone bankrupt. Katy's dream was over. Even worse – her debut album had sold less than 200 copies.

Chapter 3

Killer Queen In Training

Katy was devastated. At the tender age of 17, how could her career already be over?

The biggest disappointment that she had faced was watching her record label crash and burn. Perhaps it was inevitable. According to Christian music journalist Matthew Turner, the label had suffered from both inexperience and an ill-fated relationship with money. "Red Hill was seen as the stepchild of the Christian music labels," he claimed. "At first the label had money, but they didn't know how to spend it and ended up wasting a lot. It wasn't around long."

Red Hill was also somewhat isolated from its competitors. At that time, most Christian labels had a partnership under the umbrella of a mainstream record label. For instance, Chordant had teamed up with EMI, Provident with Sony and Ward with Warner. The backing of a major label would help guarantee distribution to stores, transforming them from tiny, little known start-ups into widely available names. Yet Red Hill had chosen to separate itself from the mainstream altogether and seek independence, associating itself exclusively with music that carried a Christian message. Whether the decision was motivated by moral beliefs or simply a desire to stand alone, it backfired miserably.

"The label was well-funded but we lacked adequate distribution," Philip Von Wrede told the author. "During that time, most of the large Christian distributors had distribution in the Christian market as well as the general market. We were a start-up and had the desire to create our own distribution which only served the Christian market. Being that most pop-oriented Christian artists were being pushed by the top three distributors, we'd always get last priority as far as retail. In my opinion, Pamplin Records [parent company of Red Hill], which was started with 20 million dollars and ongoing financial support, would've had much more success if they would have remained with Chordant/EMI whom they were originally with. Katy's first obstacle would be to get Christian retail stores to bring in her album and get retail positioning."

Yet that was far from her only concern. "Her second obstacle was that her sound didn't really resonate with who she was," he lamented. According to him, Christian appetites craved gospel classics and Katy's brand of alternative rock simply confused them. Her songs might have had a Christian message, but they certainly didn't gel with a conventional Christian sound.

Journalist DeWayne Hamby was expecting the angelic voice of a typical Christian girl to flow from his speakers when her CD first arrived on his doorstep, but he couldn't have been more surprised. "When her first album came, I had in mind a 16-year-old light pop music vibe, as was common at that time," he told the author. "Katy's record, however, had rock elements and her voice was rich and deep. In my interview with her, I told her the record took me by surprise."

Katy was already standing out as an unusual artist. It wasn't merely a question of taste though – some hard-line Christians equated pounding rock beats with Satan himself. "People are just hearing a rhythm they like when they listen to rock," an anonymous blogger complained. "It's so far removed from God that it diverts attention from the real message."

However, Jay Swartzendruber, the former editor of *Christian Music Today* and a man who had also interviewed Katy, disagreed. He told the *Christian Post*: "The greatest gift for my faith has been music and that's been rock music, quite frankly. It is artists using rock music to present a Christian worldview." He added: "I think that we are on very dangerous territory when we credit the devil for creating something. The devil is a perverter and a distorter. He does not create. God is the creator of music. To say that a style of music is evil based only on the way it sounds... we are calling the devil a creator. I think that is really dicey ground to be walking on."

Another issue was that, in the eyes of the public, Katy might have lacked authenticity. Not only was her music rocky and some of her lyrics controversial, she had readily admitted that she had got into music just because she craved people's attention – and singing had proved the most effective way to get it. She had confessed that her mother had dragged her to sing in church during her childhood, when she would rather have been elsewhere.

Even now that the reluctance had faded and music had become her primary focus in life by choice, she seemed far from sure about her subject matter. In fact, at the very moment she landed her record deal, she had already started to veer away from God. "When I first got signed... to tell you the truth, I was starting to pull away from Christianity a bit because there was too much emphasis on how other people were doing wrong," Katy told *Christian Contemporary Music*. "I think a lot of people go through a period like that in life. Romans says that the most important thing is faith. If everyone had to follow the law 100% to be saved, no-one would be saved. So here I was kind of questioning and then the owner of the label says he wants me to sing at his church!"

At this time of uncertainty, Katy had just been asked to write an album full of songs that proclaimed her love for God. Could it be that, because she was questioning the very meaning and relevance of religion by then, her songs came across as half-hearted? After all, how could she reach her target market when she no longer shared their belief system, was no longer part of it?

Katy contradicted herself by telling the media at that time that her faith had become her own and that it was no longer a case of following family tradition. However, as an insecure teenager, was she simply looking to gain approval? Whatever the truth was, her onlookers were already beginning to doubt whether she was an authentic Christian.

Besides that, Katy's quirky personality didn't fit the mould of the typical God-fearing artist either. Her then publicist, Mandy Collinger-

Parsons, revealed: "Katy was very raw and had a strong personality with no preconceived notions of what she should say or how she should act. She was transparent, to her detriment at times, and we really had to work on finessing her speech and behaviour a bit."

Yet despite the lessons in etiquette and PR presentation, when Katy arrived in the interview room, it was as if none of that had ever happened. Before long, her big-mouth reputation started to precede her.

"She was never a butt-kisser," Mandy continued. "She didn't give the rehearsed answer; she said what was on her mind. She didn't have much of a filter, nor was she always eloquent and I think this probably put off a lot of media that was used to more traditional interviews. The people who got her were few and far between."

Journalist Matthew Turner concurred, telling the author: "Though most of her official answers seemed framed by people who were trying to shape her career, I could tell that Katy didn't mind fudging the rules and speaking her own mind. She was independent and confident. A more conservative Christian might describe her demeanour as rebellious."

Katy was also willing to be naughty and unsophisticated. "There was a moment in my interview where I used the word 'shitty' to describe a situation," Matthew continued. "She immediately stood up and gave me a high five. That almost seemed to make her trust me a bit more. I could tell she didn't exactly fit the Christian music mould, that she was looking for something more."

The Christian climate certainly had restrictions for Katy. Traditionally it had proved difficult for female artists to make it in the genre – but even more so for feisty, outspoken ones who couldn't – or wouldn't – conform to the desired image of bashful innocence. "Back then, it was difficult for female artists to break into the industry," Matthew explained. "It was still a male-dominated world – especially at Christian radio. And because she was a rock chick, her style of music didn't fit into the genre of chick music that Christian radio DJs were playing at the time."

And while female gospel artists were expected to be demure and well-behaved and the picture of femininity, Katy struggled with that persona too. "She was a tomboy and she talked tough," Matthew recalled. "She also talked about boys a lot. She was quirky and unafraid to march to her own beat." What was more, there were already murmurings that Katy's sound might have been more suited to the mainstream, although gospel was the direction her parents were urging her to take.

Russ Breimeier told the author: "Her debut was different from other Christian artists. It sounded more current and accessible – a Christian release that could be more meaningful and relevant to the mainstream." Katy wasn't exactly off-key with the genre – she was more out of tune.

While Katy might have been more cut out for a different genre, it seemed that, for all her bravado, she lacked the confidence to realise that. She struggled to present herself in front of a camera and, according to Russ, "didn't endear herself to media or retail".

"I guess some artists talk the talk and walk the walk more when it comes to Christian music," he claimed. "They say the right things that radio and retail expect to hear and they fit in more with the scene – there is a tendency to produce cookie-cutter artists in the gospel music industry. I welcome a little bit of quirkiness and individuality when it comes to artists – the things that help set someone apart and make them personable. Katy had those qualities but she went too far with them."

Philip Von Wrede blamed inexperience for her controversial public persona, insisting: "I think she was a teenager that was sheltered and felt awkward when it came to speaking on camera."

Indeed, although she appeared self-assured in some areas of her life, she was still growing as a person and – far from the glamour puss she would soon become – she could be shy and reserved. Whatever her message was, she had been plunged into the public eye at a time when she didn't feel comfortable enough to express her true message – or, perhaps, even to be honest with herself about what that message could be.

DeWayne Hamby clarified: "She was ahead of her time. As she was so young when she started in the business, she was susceptible to being misled and needed guidance. I met her at 16. Even though she was wise beyond her years, she was set up for a huge let-down at a young age."

While some of her interviewers might have seen her as an awkward, ill-prepared teenager without the skills to embrace fame, others had a different view of her. According to Mark Moring of *Christianity Today*, she was a "care-free spirit who loved her music and loved people. She was very gregarious and outgoing – the word shy would not apply to her in the least."

Meanwhile Russ Breimeier saw a side of her that did not emerge in public until several years later. "Suffice to say, I've heard she was goofy, flirtatious and willing to do anything for attention," he said.

Not only was Katy an enigma with her fair share of contradictions, she was counter-cultural and ill-fitted to her genre – and she knew it. However, perhaps there was an opening for a spokesperson for torn teenagers – those who wanted to embrace Christianity but were challenged by it. She might have provided a voice for people who related to her struggle to be a good Christian, but came into conflict with that ambition while trying their best to follow the rules. Katy had already known beyond all doubt that she had a dark side. She told *Christian Contemporary Music* of her performances: "People appreciate knowing that underneath all the candy-coated frosting, there's a burnt inside."

Perhaps if her label had survived, she could have become that mentor, but she was instead facing the fact that her gospel career was now nothing more than a broken dream. "At the time I was so jazzed," Katy told *The New York Times*. "I wanted to be [gospel singer] Amy Grant." Amy had been one of the first Christian artists to achieve widespread mainstream success, winning a Grammy for Best Contemporary Gospel Performance in 1985. The same year, her album became the first gospel CD by a solo artist to go gold in the sales ranks. Following that, she decided to cross over into the world of secular pop, causing her fans to speculate whether an unusually "saucy" leopard-print jacket was an immodest way to dress on an album cover.

The two had more in common than just a penchant for leopard print though. Like Katy, Amy had also been offered a recording contract in her mid teens. Katy idolised her, so when she didn't achieve the dizzying heights of success enjoyed by Amy in her Christian career, she borrowed another one of her career moves – switching over to pop.

The transition was simple. After dismissal from her label, Katy had begun to record some demos with a new producer who encouraged her to rethink her sound. "Growing up, I wasn't really allowed to listen to a whole lot of what my mom would call secular music, so I didn't have a whole lot of references," she told *Star Scoop*. "When the producer I was doing my demos with was like, 'OK, so who would you want to work with if you could work with anybody?', I was like, 'I really have no idea.'"

Up to that point, Katy's only experience of popular music had been donning headphones and burying herself under the bed covers to muffle the sound. She would even cram her duvet into the crack underneath her door to make doubly sure that the sound wouldn't escape. Under her mother's watchful eye, it had been more of a guilty secret than a pleasure. Plus, as far as chart music was concerned, she was a total beginner.

Shamefaced, she returned to her hotel room that night and switched on a previously forbidden music channel – VH1. "I turned on VH1 and saw Glen Ballard talking about Alanis Morissette," she recalled. "I thought, 'You know what? I want to work with him!'"

To Katy, Alanis was like a "fly on every girl's wall" so she was the ideal idol for someone who, as far as the life of an average teenager was concerned, was totally out of the loop. She wanted to be that relevant, that modern and that relatable in her own music. Could working with Glen break the religion barrier and transform her into someone cool and chic?

He had certainly found Alanis success. After working with her on the album *Jagged Little Pill*, it had exceeded all expectations, going 16 times platinum in the USA alone and selling over 30 million copies. Another of Katy's idols, the group No Doubt, had also achieved multi-platinum status under Glen's wing with their album *Return To Saturn*. His other accolades included co-producing three of Michael Jackson's albums – *Thriller, Bad* and *Dangerous* – and subsequently working with Christina Aguilera, Aerosmith and Shakira. During this time, music industry legend Quincy Jones had named Glen "the ideal producer".

Aside from his glowing references, his track record spoke for itself – Glen had clocked up six Grammy awards and sales of nearly 150 million records. On paper, his success dwarfed that of most of the artists he'd written for.

While working with Glen was no guarantee of success, Katy felt it was her best shot. She told her producer, who pulled all the strings to arrange a meeting with him. Her heart was pounding on the day of her audition.

Her confidence had been knocked by the failure of her first album, so she wasn't optimistic about a call back. She was so convinced that her endeavour would end in failure that she even asked her father, who had driven her there, to leave the engine running.

"I said, 'Dad, stay in the car,'" she told *Star Scoop*. "'I'm just gonna go in, play a song for this guy and come back out.' And I guess it went well, because I got the call the next day."

Katy was exactly what Glen had been looking for. "Great voices are to me like great paintings," he explained. "They're very rare and they should be treasured because 10 million people go by and then 10 million and one, God says, 'You get a great voice.' And then another 10 million go by. So my whole life has been about finding the voices for my songs."

He had been waiting for someone who matched his work, a Cinderella to fit the precisely measured glass slipper – and, as a poverty-stricken yet hardy and determined young star in the making, Katy fit the bill. Sensing there was something special about her that couldn't easily be replicated in other artists, he put all of his faith in her and invited her to relocate to LA. The words he seduced Katy with? "I want to help you make all your dreams come true."

There was no promise of a record deal, but it was a golden opportunity to make connections and get back into the music industry – and Katy leapt at the chance. Her parents were equally thrilled, granting her permission to leave on one condition – that she finished school first. Agitated and on a mission to get her musical career back on the road, Katy finished her GED – the American equivalent of GCSEs – in record-breaking time. She graduated early, in the first term of her freshman year. As a parting shot, she left Santa Barbara in style, telling *MTV*: "I went to homecoming with a senior and that made me feel really cool because when you catch a senior for homecoming or for prom or whatever it is, you made it."

Now that Katy had finished school, she turned her attention back to her musical education, listening to Glen's songs over and over again. An anonymous friend told the author: "I think it was like landing on Mars for Katy – it was a whole new world to her. Can you believe that, unlike almost every other high school kid, she'd never heard Michael Jackson before?"

She might have been the butt of jokes with her classmates, but all that was about to change. Armed with a handful of her favourite pop-music albums and a brand-new car, Katy left her hometown to carve out a new life for herself in LA. It was a testing time – would she end up on the "boulevard of broken dreams" or would she join the ranks of the city's most glamorous stars? Only time would tell.

On arrival in the big city, her outlook on life instantly began to change. "The things that I thought when I was 15 or 16 didn't make sense [later] just because my perspective had changed. I'd seen more of the world," she told *The Scotsman*. "I'd lived more of life and met more different types of people. When I started out in my gospel music, my perspective then was a bit enclosed and very strict and everything I had in my life at that time was church-related. I didn't know there was another world that existed beyond that. So when I left home and saw all of that, it was like, 'Ohmigosh, I fell down the rabbit hole and there's this whole Alice in Wonderland right there!'"

Katy's wonderland included her boyfriend Matt Thiessen, whom she had met on the Christian touring circuit. He too was counter-cultural, with his band Relient K described by critics as "the sounds of a secular rock group". Both intended to live according to God's law, but when the two were let loose to explore the bright lights of LA, disaster struck – Katy lost her virginity.

After pledging to wait until marriage, she had allowed temptation to get the better of her one night. "My boyfriend and I went a little too far and I felt I'd fallen so far away from God," Katy lamented to *Seventeen*. "I doubted myself and my strength. I was so weak at the time in my relationship with Christ."

Those who had listened hard to her first album might have wondered whether it was the premarital sex that she felt guilty about, or simply the infidelity to her romantic fantasy relationship with God.

That night, Katy had broken two major rules – not only was she having sex, but it was to the tune of a secular soundtrack – Jeff Buckley's *Grace*. Teasingly, she recalled that the album had been "better than the sex".

However, the guilt she had felt over their first sexual tryst was soon abandoned. She laughed it off when *Stepping Out* magazine later spotted a tell-tale ring on her finger, announcing: "They think a promise ring means no sex! No, the promise ring is just a promise that he'll get me another ring. A better ring! I say that in all sarcasm. Seriously, it's not one of those no-sex promise rings. That kind of went out the window when I was 17 years old."

After losing her virginity, Katy began to question some of the other rules of life that she'd always taken for granted. "Letting go was a process," she told *Christianity Today*. "Meeting gay people or Jewish people and realising that they were fine was a big part of it. Once I stopped being chaperoned and realised I had a choice in life, I was like, 'Wow, there are a lot of choices.' I began to become a sponge for all that I had missed... I was as curious as the cat. But I'm not dead yet."

However, it raised some awkward questions for Katy, bringing her beliefs into direct conflict with both the teachings of the Bible and the house rules her parents had always insisted on. She hadn't been allowed to take friends home for dinner unless they were fellow Christians and homosexuality was considered a sin. "I came from a strict repressed [household] where being gay was wrong," she explained.

However, some might argue that Katy's beliefs were not her own but inherited – and some scandals emerged that could raise a question mark over those beliefs forever.

Ted Haggard, an evangelical preacher who had appeared in the film *Jesus Camp* and who had always had an outwardly anti-gay stance, was sensationally outed as homosexual. Resignation from the pulpit swiftly followed after he was found "guilty of sexual immorality". The scandal sparked talk of hypocrisy and double standards but also raised the question: was homosexuality really so wrong?

Subsequently Hopeline, the Christian phone service that Katy had written about in her gospel song 'Last Call' after reading a book by its founder, was embroiled in an equally grisly scandal. A teenager had phoned in posing as a teenager unsure of his sexuality and had been told that if he embraced God, he could be "cured". The adviser also made parallels between homosexuality and drug addiction, alcoholism and pornography. The disgusted teenager later blogged: "Despicable. Can you imagine the number of gay or questioning children that, because of this advice, have hurt or killed themselves?"

A nation was outraged – and an uncomfortable Katy was forced to question the rules of her faith. At around this time, she met and teamed up with a rapper – also from a strict religious background – who was able to help clear her head. That rapper's name was Mickey Avalon.

Together the two wrote a song, 'High And The Lows', which expressed ideas Katy could never have dared voice to her parents. Not only did it expose what Mickey believed to be serious hypocrisy on the church scene, but it also created fictional characters who committed sins while continuing to preach the word of God.

The controversial verses included incest allegations such as "Preacher McGrath was always keen to ask why his mother rubbed her hands beneath his pants at mass". Another character, named Stephanie, was a crystal meth addict desperately trying to fight off her father's advances. Mickey rapped: "Her papa was a preacher so she knew the good book, and when he tucked her into bed, he fondled the nook... maybe she'd be in better health if her father learned to keep his hands to himself."

To add to the controversy, the song was based on imaginary calls to a Christian help hotline – just like the more innocent one Katy had penned earlier. When it reached its final verse, the troubled young caller had grown up and become a counsellor himself, breaking the cycle. The song was so controversial that it only received airplay once – on the radio show *Loveline*, where young people were encouraged to call in and confess their darkest secrets.

Mickey himself had seemed a good contender for a distressed caller on one of these shows, as his own childhood had been a textbook case of turbulence.

Although he had begun life as a strictly religious Jew, he had experienced a colourful lifestyle. He'd grown up with a heroin-addicted father and a drug-dealer mother, a career which he later took on for himself. His murky past included drug addiction, depression and financial struggle – and critics had suggested that some of the subject matter in the song was autobiographical. While no-one was surprised by his satire, the biggest scandal was God-fearing Katy's participation.

For her, the tune offered the opportunity to hold a mirror up to the ills of society, parodying them in the process – but her family might not have been so sympathetic.

"To this day I am still the black sheep of the family," Katy later told *The Scotsman*. "They're used to my dark sense of humour and my thick layer of sarcasm, which is slapped on everything. Even though I've had a strict Christian upbringing, they've always known that about me – and I'm sure it became more fully fledged when I left the nest."

While the tune might have suited her dark sense of humour, fans of her previous work tended to find it tasteless. One thing was for sure – the ironic, bitterly sarcastic lyrics were already further away from her gospel past than anyone could have imagined.

Katy's recording sessions with Glen Ballard also captured the gulf between her past and her present. In 'Rock God', she apologies for allowing music to replace Christ as her new religion. She expresses sorrow for leaving the angels crying over her demise, but protests that her love of a good beat is hurting no-one. "Father, I'm torn, selling my soul to the rhythm, the beat and the bass, cuz I can't confess my rock 'n' roll ways," she sings.

The song first took shape while Katy was working with an old friend and songwriter named Printz Board. The two hit it off when Printz unwittingly sang a line from a song that exactly described her childhood. That song was 'Son Of A Preacher Man' – originally performed by Dusty Springfield, and recorded for her landmark 1969 album *Dusty In Memphis*.

It explained, like 'Rock God', how being good "wasn't always easy" as the writer was infatuated with music. In fact, it became just as much his calling as God had once been. Katy had squealed, "Wait, I like that – that sounds like my story!" on hearing Printz's rendition. Inspired, the two instantly started recording.

"I went into the booth and just said, 'Press record,'" Printz told the author. "I did this crazy vocal intro that was like, 'Yo, yo, yo, this is Katy Perry and Printz Board – WHAAAAT???!' I came out of the booth laughing my head off and she said, 'Keep it! I love it!' That might've been the moment that I fell in love with her – she's just amazing and I'm glad to just be her friend."

Katy had found it easier to work with someone she already knew – she had met Printz the previous year through a mutual friend, James Valentine, the guitarist in Maroon 5. The feeling was mutual with Printz describing Katy as a "ball of energy in the studio".

The songwriting continued with other guests too, featuring references to the drug culture she would witness in LA and that subsequent boyfriends would fall prey to. In 'Speed Dialing', God seems almost entirely forgotten, as she talks of using the drug Novocaine to numb her heart's pain. The plot follows a lovelorn woman who drinks and dials after a night out because she misses her ex-lover.

Meanwhile, the tune 'In Between' hits out at a man who sees her as no more than a one-night stand. The all or nothing ultimatum with its gritty honesty betrays traces of Fiona Apple or Alanis Morissette – but, more intriguingly, it seems to portray an increasingly party-prone Katy losing her religion.

'The Box', co-written with Matt Thiessen, illustrates her transition perfectly. "I started living outside of the box, crossing over lines where I always used to stop," she sings, "cuz I'm not gonna be anybody that I'm not."

This tendency to break boundaries had been part of Katy's nature since childhood. "If there was [ever] a line you shouldn't cross, I would take a big leap over it," she told *Artist Direct*. "There is not an edit button on my keyboard of life."

However, now that Katy had fled her hometown, she was taking her indiscretions one step further. "Then it hit me," she sings. "You won't permit me, to be an individual, just doesn't fit me, but I decided that's no way to be living…Yeah, I decided I'm escaping from your prison." Is the song an ode to her upbringing?

If so, the song 'It's Okay To Believe' reflects some uncertainty about her decision to break free, asking why she perpetually hesitates before letting her "cocoon break".

Meanwhile, in 'Diamonds', she compares herself to a pebble drowning in the ocean, fretting over the pressure piled onto her as she looks for fame. However, her ambition is to transform from that dirty diamond in the rough to a gleaming gem – if she manages it, she concludes, all of her work will have been worthwhile.

However, like most journeys to success, the story also has a dark side. 'Wish You The Worst' is a dose of Ashley Simpson-style straight-talking, telling the story of a jilted ex-girlfriend dead set on revenge. The lyrics sneer: "Let me be the curse that creeps under your skin, until your heart caves in and you wish she was me again."

Katy lightened the mood during rehearsal time by dedicating the words to a cat that had slept on her bed while suffering from a stomach upset and had left an unwelcome gift by her pillow for when she woke up.

In direct contrast to some of Katy's more liberated early songs, 'I Do Not Hook Up' is a loud and proud proclamation of celibacy. Here, she tells her boyfriend in no uncertain terms that she wants to take it slow.

Meanwhile, another tune, 'It Takes One To Know One', berates an ex for his infidelity. It appears to borrow the phrase "You thought I'd cry, you thought I'd lay down and die" from disco queen Gloria Gaynor, but the mood is a little darker.

Her work with Glen also captured some tender moments. As if exhausted by all the angst, Katy gives in to love on 'The Better Half Of Me'. She puts a partner whom she had previously "taken advantage of" and used to climb the ladder out of his misery, insisting that she has had enough of the game-playing and that, without him, life "has no value".

A love-struck Katy learns to trust again in the similarly themed 'Longshot', where the accompanying video sees her gaze romantically into the eyes of Matt Thiessen and pledge to take a chance on love. Yet it was also about gathering enough faith to dare to believe she could make it in music, despite the adversity.

Katy's good girl persona was still revealing itself at times. Her solace in desperate moments comes not from a cold beer or a line of cocaine like some of her musical counterparts, but from a wholesome cup of coffee. In the song 'Cup Of Coffee', she makes it clear it's the only thing she's likely to overdose on. Perhaps she took her parents' warning not to turn into Amy Winehouse to heart.

Other tunes that Katy and Glen brought to life included 'Weigh Me Down', 'Oh Love Let Me Sleep', 'LA Don't Take It Away' and – one of Katy's personal favourites – 'Sherlock Holmes'. However, the tune

'Simple' is the most revealing of 17-year-old Katy's life. It has the modern references she had longed for, name-checking distressed jeans and Louis Vuitton handbags as signatures of the modern secular lifestyle to which she'd only just found the key.

The song is a candid story of Katy's life, telling of a girl so insecure that she sleeps with the lights on, just as she had written about in 'My Own Monster'. It tells of someone whose lifestyle leads to financial ruin. For Katy it was a will to succeed in music and the expensive gamble that followed, while for her character it was an obsession with designer threads. The jibe "You park in a loading zone" was an ode to the self-inflicted obstacles that littered her path to success.

Indeed, there would be many obstacles to come. Despite penning dozens of tunes with one of the most successful producers in the country, even that couldn't guarantee Katy success. Island Def Jam briefly signed her in 2003, but struggled to find a way to market the would-be starlet.

"It was definitely an issue to promote Katy," an anonymous employee revealed. "Certain people felt that she had one foot in the gospel camp, which we knew very little about, and one foot in the pop and rock camp. I know it sounds bad to say an artist needs to be manufactured by skilled people to get success, but I doubt if even Katy knew who or what she was."

While there was an opening for a feisty pop artist, the label began to doubt whether Katy was the right person to fit it. "There was definitely potential there, otherwise we would never have pursued it," the employee continued, "but she had to grow into her image and sound a bit first."

While she was trying her best to do that, the label pulled the plug on her debut and her journey to the top seemed ever more hopeless.

Next she signed to Columbia in 2004, but again she encountered people who were even stronger-willed than herself. Released from the restrictive ties of trying to be a good girl in a gospel environment, Katy had come out of her shell and her own creative vision had begun to emerge. Yet it was a case of finding the right label – one that would encourage her proactive participation – because Katy didn't want to be manufactured. Yet tragically she was finding it increasingly difficult to hold on to a record deal at all.

At least her experience with Columbia had been less humiliating than with Island Def Jam. The latter had told Katy, along with three other girls who had been signed at the same time: "Maybe one of you will ever make a record. The other three can go back to middle America and pop out babies."

After the decision to shelve the album, her life became a blur of constant casting calls and auditions. She became so accustomed to hearing the word "no" that the rejections barely fazed her any more. "It's those little curve balls in life that make you stronger," she reportedly told a friend.

However, one advertisement that caught Katy's eye turned out to be a little different. Famous three-piece songwriting team The Matrix was looking for a male and female duo to front a new band and an increasingly desperate Katy was one of the first in the queue to audition.

The group had a reputation for taking failed artists who had no hope and transforming them into world-famous platinum-selling stars. For frontwoman Lauren Christy, it had all begun with a desire to be famous. Yet, after two failed albums, she was dropped by her label. Like Katy, she then suffered rejection after rejection in her bid for success. The last straw was when she flew all the way to London from her home in LA to meet a talent scout. He decided against signing her, but – as a parting shot – asked her manager, "Can I have a song of hers to use for Natalie Imbruglia's next single?"

Wounded by the slight, Lauren decided in that moment that the fame game was over for her. Vowing never to seek a record deal again, she joined forces with her husband, Graham Edwards, whose band Dollshead had just been dropped by its label too. Together with his keyboardist, Scott Spock, the three hatched a plan. They would stop chasing the increasingly elusive success they had dreamed of and instead do what they loved best behind the scenes. They might not have been marketable by themselves, but perhaps they could mastermind other people's careers. Using its name as a euphemism for a womb, The Matrix wanted to be the life force where all songs began.

Together, the three helped Christina Aguilera, Busted, David Bowie, Ricky Martin and Britney Spears find or rediscover success, winning a

KATY PREPARES TO SWEET-TALK GOSSIP COLUMNIST AND MUSIC CRITIC PEREZ HILTON AT HIS 30TH BIRTHDAY PARTY ON MARCH 22, 2008 AT THE BEVERLY WILSHIRE HOTEL IN LOS ANGELES, ARRIVING WITH A FLOWER IN HER HAIR. (RYAN BORN/WIREIMAGE)

THE CENTRE OF ATTENTION AS ALWAYS, AN OUTLANDISH KATY EARNS ADMIRING GLANCES FROM HER MORE CONSERVATIVE BAND MEMBERS IN THE MATRIX AS THE GROUP HIT THE RECORDING STUDIO. (IANWHITE.COM/CORBIS)

KATY SOAKS UP THE LIMELIGHT AT ONE OF HER EARLIER SHOWS, PERFORMING FOR THE Q102 JUNGLE BALL AT THE SUSQUEHANNA BANK CENTER IN CAMDEN, NEW JERSEY, ON DECEMBER 14, 2008. (JEFF FUSCO/GETTY IMAGES)

KATY STRUGGLES UNDER THE WEIGHT OF TWO MTV GONGS AS SHE ADVERTISES THE 2009 EUROPE MUSIC AWARDS IN BERLIN AND PREPARES TO HOST THE CEREMONY. (DAVE HOGAN/GETTY IMAGES)

NO ORDINARY STAGE SHOW: PINK INFLATABLE FLAMINGOS AND HEART-SHAPED SUNGLASSES ARE JUST A NORMAL PART OF THE ACTION FOR KATY AS SHE PERFORMS AT THE T IN THE PARK FESTIVAL IN KINROSS, SCOTLAND ON JULY II, 2008. (BRIAN SWEENEY/GETTY IMAGES)

WHOEVER COINED THE PHRASE "LIKE MOTHER, LIKE DAUGHTER" HAD OBVIOUSLY NEVER MET KATY PERRY. HERE, KATY SHARES THE SPOTLIGHT WITH HER DEEPLY RELIGIOUS MOTHER AS THE TWO WORK THE CROWD FOR HER *ONE OF THE BOYS* ALBUM LAUNCH PARTY IN LA ON JUNE 17, 2008. (JESSE GRANT/GETTY IMAGES FOR EMI MUSIC)

YOUNG LOVE: KATY POSES FOR THE CAMERA AT THE MTV VIDEO MUSIC AWARDS IN LA ON SEPTEMBER 7, 2008 WITH HER THEN BEAU, TRAVIS McCOY. (CHIRS POLK/FILM MAGIC)

KATY, PICTURED WITH PEREZ HILTON, DONS THE TRADEMARK MOUSTACHE OF HER IDOL FREDDIE MERCURY, AS THE TWO ATTEND HER 24TH BIRTHDAY PARTY ON OCTOBER 28, 2008 AT LA'S SIREN STUDIOS. PEREZ WENT ON TO COPY THE CROSS-DRESSING STUNT, APPEARING AT A SUBSEQUENT PARTY AS LADY GA
(ALEXANDRA WYMAN/WIREIMAGE)

KATY COMPETES WITH LADY GAGA IN THE STYLE STAKES BY DONNING A DECK OF CARDS IN HER HAIR AS SHE POSES WITH HER GRANDMOTHER FOR
THE ROC LAS VEGAS LAUNCH PARTY AT THE NEW YORK HOTEL AND CASINO IN LAS VEGAS, ON AUGUST 30, 2008.
(DENISE TRUSCELLO/WIREIMAGE)

INSPIRED BY A RECENT TRIP TO INDIA, DURING WHICH RUSSELL BRAND PROPOSED, KATY APPEARS UNUSUALLY DRESSED DOWN IN TRADITIONAL HINDU GARB AND FACE JEWEL, AS SHE POSES WITH HER LOVER AT LA'S 2010 GRAMMY AWARDS ON JANUARY 31. (LARRY BUSACCA/GERRY IMAGES FOR NARA

string of awards and seven Grammy nominations. Fame might not have taken the shape the three had imagined, but they were now household names in the music industry.

In 2004, they were approached by Sony Records to develop a band for them, and consider stepping out of the shadows to co-front it themselves. Lauren jumped at the chance. "They wanted an album by The Matrix, so we did it," she told *Songwriter Universe*. "It would feature a young male singer and a young female singer, like Fleetwood Mac. Our intention was that we would stay behind the scenes, with the two lead singers out in front. But as things evolved, Sony said they wanted to include us."

Lauren added to *INK19* magazine: "We like being behind the scenes and we thought, 'Well, for five years we've been behind the scenes doing our own thing very happily and someone is offering us a chance to literally go in and be creative. From our own point of view, rather than always trying to get across another artist's point of view. It was just interesting for the three of us to say, 'What do WE actually want to say?' I think it would be sad to turn your back on an experience that is offered to you, so we just said yes."

Auditions began in earnest. Adam Longlands, a young amateur, clinched the group's male role, while Katy was chosen as the female face. Columbia had provided a glowing reference to aid that process.

Katy was fascinated by The Matrix. They had gone from struggling hopefuls who could barely earn a living to world-famous cutting-edge songwriters in a matter of years – and Katy was heartened by that. "Our manager kept saying, 'You're going to be huge,'" Lauren recalled of her pop-star hustle. "But things wouldn't happen for us. There used to be times when the three of us were sleeping on the floor."

Katy had shared the group's poverty and hopelessness, but The Matrix had known how to turn their plight around and Katy had her fingers crossed that they could do the same for her.

The group now had an excellent track record, plucking Avril Lavigne from virtual obscurity when she had been about to get dropped from her label, and turning her into a success story, selling 12 million copies of her debut album.

The group also promised to be the antithesis of Columbia. While the latter had refused to hand over the reins to Katy, The Matrix wanted to work on equal terms to find her preferred style. Scott Spock explained to *INK19*: "We take the things that are really cool about an artist and focus on that, distilling it down to its essence without ever taking the artist out of the music."

Katy felt confident that the group wouldn't try to mould her into a generic brand of bubblegum pop. Instead, their focus was broader and they had succeeded with many genres, from candy-coated pop like Britney Spears to metal-tinged hard rock such as Korn. They ticked boxes for Katy by having produced Liz Phair, who would appeal to her love of strong women. Meanwhile Lauren's solo projects had been hailed for their similarity to Alanis Morissette. The Matrix had even excelled with the Latino rhythms of hip-shaking Shakira and Katy was confident that they not only had a broad-based knowledge of music but that they could help her find her own identity as an artist.

Tellingly, they had reinvented Avril Lavigne who was first introduced to them as a reluctant gospel music star. She had come from a religious family and, like Katy, had first performed onstage in church. While her record company had sought to turn her into a squeaky-clean pop singer, Avril loathed the likes of Faith Hill and had ambitions of becoming a punk princess instead.

The Matrix listened to her ideas and within days the group had co-written the hits 'Complicated', 'Sk8r Boi' and 'I'm With You'. The rags to riches tales of both The Matrix and the groups they had worked with inspired Katy and she was looking forward to working with them – could she finally have found her big break?

As experienced "production geniuses", The Matrix modernised Katy's approach to recording music from the start. They used cutting-edge technology whereas Katy had been strapped for cash and was using far less sophisticated equipment. "I have a four-track in the trunk of my car that I take everywhere," she confessed to *INK19* to peals of laughter from her bandmates. "Everybody's talking about gadgets and stuff like that and getting all technical and I'm like, 'Yeah, I've got a four-track that my ex-boyfriend gave me as a going-away gift that I write all my songs on.'"

The Matrix's technical expertise might have reinvented Katy's sound and taken it up another notch, but it hadn't eliminated all disasters. Katy recalled: "One evening, when we were almost finished with the whole record, when Scott got back to turn on the hard drive, six out of seven [songs] had been wiped. And we were like, 'Oh shit, are we going to have to re-record everything that we had been recording for the past five months?' Of course I've got the biggest mouth and I'm like, 'Oh my God, we've lost our record!' [But] we had some tech nerd come in and be like, 'Well, you know, all you have to do is flick this switch on and there it is.'"

The project had included four duets with co-singer Adam Longlands – 'Broken', 'You Miss Me', 'Take a Walk' and 'Stay with Me' – and three solo performances on which Katy took the lead vocals alone, 'Damn', 'Just A Song' and 'Would You Care.'

Some of the lyrics had been personalised for Katy, among them 'Would You Care', which opens with "Get used to it, Katy." However, the majority of the song appeared to deal with the possible frustrations of the Matrix team, at having been invisible writers in their career rather than sharing in their protégés' success. Lyrics included: "You're just one note in a symphony, your name won't go down in history, live on in infamy, but to the point would you care?"

Meanwhile other songs had been moulded to fit long before Katy had arrived on the scene. 'Broken', primed to be the album's first single, had already been recorded the previous year by another group, The Troys. That single, renamed 'What Do You Do', had flopped and the album associated with it had been shelved. The fate of that tune would ultimately prove to be a taste of things to come.

The first curve ball came during the recording. A scandal erupted in the media when Lauren Christy suggested that Avril Lavigne had played almost no part in creating the songs that had made her debut album into a multi-million pound hit. A furious Avril hit back, telling *The Mirror*: "What they said was incorrect. I'm a writer and I don't appreciate someone trying to take the credit away from me. It's very fucking obvious that the lyrics came from me."

Avril had implied that the songwriting team had taken credit away from her in a bid for publicity and to increase their own notoriety and success, conveniently at a time when they were starting out fronting a major project of their own. There was now controversy surrounding the CD before it had so much as hit the shelves.

Whether The Matrix found her comments embarrassing, infuriating or merely a welcome publicity stunt, as had been implied, it wasn't necessarily a good start to their album's promotion.

The Matrix lived and breathed music and clearly had the commercial knowledge to know what made a hit. Katy had once said of the trio: "They're hit-makers from the time they strum their first chord." However, now that they were taking centre stage along with Katy and Adam, they had to face the fact that they might not have been as marketable as their recruited lead singers. "We have to be honest about what we are and what The Matrix is – people who have written hit songs for other people," Lauren told *INK19*. "And to suddenly just come out as a grass-roots band that is playing little clubs everywhere and trying to be cool would be totally fake. So what we have done is write a bunch of songs that we think would be fabulous hits, put it out to media like we have with all our other songs and hopefully the public will like it. And if they do, we'll be right there to perform."

Perhaps, then, the team lacked the fashion cred and the cool image that some of their vocalists had offered. The three had little experience of being in a band. The other concern was the song they intended to use as a lead single. If it hadn't worked for The Troys, what made The Matrix believe it could work this time around?

Katy also struggled with the sneaking suspicion that she was compromising herself – she wanted to write her own material on her own terms. For all of these reasons, the album ended up self-destructing. "That was a shame," recalled Glen Ballard. "They couldn't even decide on a single. It just fell apart."

There were even tensions between Katy and the band members. When she was offered an interview slot by *Blender* magazine and lauded as "the next big thing", she wasted no opportunity to distance herself from them. "Crap! There goes my credibility," she laughed of her decision to sign with them. "They've worked with some brilliant people but also people who are barely artists at all."

Meanwhile Lauren found Katy "unsophisticated", telling her to behave in an interview with *INK19* because the magazine was "highbrow". The band then ridiculed her for not understanding what the word meant. Jokey banter or sly digs? The truth was unknown.

Despite the disagreement, one promotional video for a single had been produced, picturing Katy wearing the forties styles she had loved the most. She appeared in a cropped tartan skirt and a red knee-length pencil skirt with matching red stilettos. She was singing 'Broken', a tune with an irresistibly youthful punk sound. That would be the final video the group shot together before the album was shelved forever.

Katy hadn't given up on the music business entirely, but she was now having serious doubts. She decided to have the word Jesus tattooed on her wrist, as her father had done on no fewer than four occasions. It became her comfort blanket, a reminder of her roots. It was also a signature of where she could find love and comfort in an increasingly tough business world.

"I still have my roots," she told *CBS News*. "I knew I wanted this on me, because no matter how much changes around me, or how much I change, there's not really an eraser for this. And [every time I play the guitar], it stares right back at me. It's like, 'Remember, you came from this – and you can always go back to it.'"

Katy's critics might have wondered whether she really meant it or if, as an insecure young woman in the depths of despair, she was simply trying to convince herself of God's existence amid her agony.

She was also trying to understand where her faith positioned her when it came to searching for a record label. Fellow Christian group Sixpence None The Richer, who had achieved brief but widespread success with the hit 'Kiss Me', had once wondered the same thing. "We don't feel comfortable signing with a Christian record label, because they will try to tell us how to write our lyrics," they had mused, "and try to give our lyrics a direction rather than giving us the freedom to think about all of life under the hands of God. We're also uncomfortable with being released under the mainstream labels because they won't respect our faith. What do we do?"

That was a question on Katy's mind too – and she began to search for solace under the umbrella of Reality Carpinteria in LA.

Reality was a Christian organisation founded by a man named Tim Chaddick. Tim would have understood the meaning of Katy's tune 'Rock God' completely. He had started out in life as the son of a pastor, but had fallen prey to "the unholy trinity of sex, drugs and rock 'n' roll". As a teenager, he had become addicted to crystal meth, had seen his pregnant girlfriend get an abortion and had become the lead singer in a string of punk rock groups. After his friends persuaded him to attend a Christian event in San Jose, one of which he had formerly described as "horrifyingly cheesy", his life changed forever.

He broke down in tears after the pastor's sermon unexpectedly resonated with him and he decided to sleep in the church gym that night. Despite that, he had never pleaded, "How shall they hear without a preacher?" In that moment pledging to move away from sin, he opened a church and started Reality.

When Katy joined, the prayer meetings were still in their infant stages – but she was starting to find God again. Meanwhile Columbia Records was working with Katy to produce her album. She recorded a promotional DVD to market her work containing video clips for the songs 'Diamonds', 'The Box', 'Longshot', 'Simple', 'A Cup Of Coffee' and 'It's Okay To Believe'. For the 'Diamonds' video, Katy had even jetted off to Paris.

'Simple' also appeared on the soundtrack of the comedy film *Sisterhood Of The Travelling Pants*. The light-hearted movie takes a look at the lives of four friends who had previously spent all their time together but are now facing a summer apart. As the four go their separate ways, they find a pair of pants that, despite their varying body shapes, fit all four perfectly. They decide that they will circulate the jeans among themselves that summer, even as far afield as Mexico and Greece.

Like Katy's Jesus tattoo, the pair of jeans becomes the one force that bonds them – through ill-fated love affairs, terminal illness, family dramas and much more besides. Katy was delighted to be part of the movie.

On August 18, 2005, she even had a limited-edition album released in Japan on Columbia to test the water. It seemed as though Katy had finally found a label that believed in her. But the following year her dreams would be shattered again – and the events that followed would cause her to question her faith in God, the music business – and even herself.

Chapter 4

Sinning For Sex Appeal

I n 2006, Katy received a phone call that would rock her world – she
was being dropped by her record label yet again. In spite of the best
efforts of her mentor, Glen, all of her hard work had come to nothing.

"We tried so many labels," he told *Entertainment Weekly*. "But, you
know, it was the same with Alanis Morissette. Everybody turned her
down. And then finally Maverick puts *Jagged Little Pill* out and it's a huge
hit. I think Katy was just maybe too ahead of her time."

Yet while he still seemed convinced that she had a chance, Katy herself
wasn't quite so sure. For the first time ever, she doubted herself and
considered giving up and going home. "It turned into a situation where
for years I was telling my friends that I was going to have a record out
– like I had the CD art and everything – and then it wouldn't happen,"
she shuddered. "I was pretty much a joke."

For Katy, who prided herself on being a strong, independent woman,
the burden was almost too much to bear. The near-misses had been
humiliating. Now, not only did her friends not believe in her, but Katy
didn't believe in herself.

Before long, she began drowning her sorrows on the LA party scene.
She was drinking heavily and spending all night dancing – and those
who had followed her gospel career didn't approve. Although she had

sold little more than 200 copies of her Christian album, she had a very big audience watching her fail. That was when the true meaning of future songs like 'Lost' really came into play.

Russ Breimeier told the author: "'Lost' certainly reads like an autobiography of her party lifestyle, doesn't it? But I think the guidance has always been there if she wanted it. She comes from a Christian family and since she was raised in the faith, she knows where to go for spiritual direction. We all feel lost sometimes and need guidance, but there's always a place we can turn to – the first step is always ours. As the old saying goes, 'If God seems far away, guess who moved?'"

Indeed, Katy confessed that she was so disheartened by her near-misses that she had put down her Bible and started to lose faith altogether. "My music wasn't happening," she told *Christian Music Central*. "I just felt kind of slow in everything and my relationship with God slowed down. I didn't crack my Bible for months."

Russ wasn't sympathetic, insisting, "If someone is going to downplay or shun their faith due to the failure of their album, perhaps their faith wasn't so strong to begin with."

To make matters worse, Katy was running out of money. She'd had to repay advances to her label when the deal turned sour, and her beloved car – an essential for attending auditions and traversing California – was repossessed. While waiting for the wheel of fortune to turn her way again, she appeared in a video for rock band P.O.D to promote the single 'Goodbye For Now'. She also made a short cameo appearance in the video 'Learn To Fly' by Carbon Leaf, contacts she had made via Glen.

However, she had to face facts – she was living in downtown LA by herself and these occasional pieces of work would never pay the bills. It added to Katy's humiliation when she wrote cheques that bounced. "I'd write cheques and in the memo section, I'd write 'Please God!'" she joked to *E! Entertainment*. "My Rolodex was filled with numbers to the brim, so why isn't this happening? I said to myself, 'If I don't make it by 25, I'm gonna refocus.'"

She had begun to refocus already, while fending off her parents' anxious phone calls. "I was broke as a joke [with] my parents calling me saying, 'What are you doing? Come home!' and I would say, 'Just wait! Just wait! Give me another month!'" she recalled.

"I came close to quitting when I couldn't pay my bills. When I had already been through being on a big label and them telling me, 'You're going to have a record out' and then finally there would be complete silence," she told *Star Pulse*, reliving the agony. "That ultimately meant that it wasn't happening after all the hard work that I put into it. It's like completing your debut movie and it never being able to come out, it's all you worked on in life."

She realised that if she wanted to continue pursuing her dream for even a month, let alone until she was 25, then she would need to take a day job. She joined Taxi Music, an independent A&R company in the upmarket suburb of Calabasas. The area was deceptively beautiful as, for Katy, going to work was a torturous nightmare, a daily reminder of how she still hadn't made it.

The company aimed to help amateur musicians make it in the industry by introducing them to publishers and record labels and giving them the advice they needed to improve their tunes. Ironically, Katy was critiquing and mentoring failed artists, when she was a failed artist herself.

She told *The Guardian*: "That was the most depressing moment of my hustle. I was sitting there in a cubicle with 25 other trying-to-make-it failed artists in a box listening to the worst music you've ever heard in your entire life. Having no money, writing bad cheques, renting a car after two cars had been repossessed, trying to give people constructive criticism and hope, when all I really wanted was to jump out of the building or cut my ears off and say, 'I can't help you! I can't catch a break. What am I gonna say to you? And you sing out of tune.'"

She added to *Seventeen*: "You have to imagine how depressed I was after not making it in LA after five years, knowing everyone in the music industry couldn't get a break. I would tell these people, 'Well, you have to change these chords' or, 'This is how you contact a record label.' And I was like, 'I cannot give these people hope.' I had no hope myself."

Seeing so many fail frightened Katy. "I saw the other girls come and go [and] I wondered if there would still be space for me," she recalled.

What was more, at that time hordes of bloggers from across the country had begun to publicly denounce Taxi, branding it a fraud. One frustrated customer claimed: "Over the course of 12 years and 100+ forwarded [song] submissions, with $3,525 spent on membership and submission fees alone, I haven't made a single deal through Taxi." However, he went on to claim that he had signed a publishing deal with a major cable network, which regularly played his songs. The implication was that Taxi could not help even the talented become successful.

While even publishers were stepping out of the shadows to criticise the company as "worthless", a journalist from *Music Thinktank* argued: "If you're young and attractive with a radio-friendly sound, a large following, verifiable sales and touring experience, Taxi might be able to hook you up with a label. But with all that going for you, do you really need them?"

Katy would echo that argument. She felt she was giving career advice to people who could barely sing, when she had spectacularly failed with her own career. Critics might have argued that amateurs would prefer to receive advice from experienced veterans in the industry who already knew about success. For Katy, the very meaning of the word was elusive.

During that dark period of her life, she auditioned for Capitol Records, which initially expressed interest but then also declined her. She swallowed her pride and started recording again, determined to find the perfect song that would win her a record deal.

During that time, she endured catty comments from others in the business. "I had someone say to me, 'Psst, you should probably go home, because you've never gonna get signed again. You're pretty much damaged goods, and you should be in the defect aisle [at the supermarket],'" she told *Entertainment Weekly*. "And I'm 20 at that point. I'm like, 'I'm defective goods already?'"

Katy was incredulous, but Glen Ballard offered her some fatherly advice. "I encouraged Katy not so much to rebel against anything she's been through but to actually use it towards defining who she was as a person," he recalled. Perhaps it was this piece of advice that changed Katy's public persona altogether. Who was she as a person? Onlookers were about to find out.

Katy began to record some new songs, the most dramatic of which was 'All I'm Selling Is Sex'. The track had references to prostitution, casual sex and posing naked, including the lyrics, "I'm a lady, good for one thing maybe... will you be my sugar daddy if I promise to behave? Then you can have me, but you'll be digging your own grave."

This dangerous femme fatale persona that Katy was portraying was no longer playful and teasing, but raw, unadulterated sexuality. Listeners also learned that Katy was willing to bathe in champagne to promote the song. Since she had told *Blender* that she would "do anything for attention", that didn't seem unlikely.

According to one anonymous acquaintance, her attitude was no surprise. "Katy wanted to make it big no matter what – at any cost – and if she lost her dignity in the process, then so be it," he claimed. "She didn't care what she was famous for as long as she was famous. She has always longed to be noticed – in any crowd, she would be the loudest, quirkiest and most willing to shock."

He added, "She fell into Christian music because she thought it's what she could succeed at, using her parents' connections. She wasn't exactly friends with Gwen Stefani at the time, was she? But her parents knew plenty of gospel music guys, so it seemed the best way to go. Her family was strong and united so she knew she could rely on their support even if she went against their wishes. I think that it was having so much unconditional love at home that actually gave her the confidence to turn against what she was taught. Looking at what she's doing now, it's hard to believe she ever took God seriously. If she was asked to get up on that stage and sing odes to Satan, I think she would have done it."

These were harsh words for Katy. Perhaps the failure of her Christian album had made her think that, if she wanted to go for global domination in the music world, then she had to sacrifice religion and be palatable to the mainstream, satisfying their appetite for salacious stories. After all, Charlotte Church and Avril Lavigne had only become household names when they ditched the choir-girl connotations and started making music for the masses.

On the other hand, perhaps this new liberated self was what Katy had craved all along, but it wasn't until now that she'd had the confidence to express it. Either way, if she'd set out to shock and confuse, that was exactly the effect she'd been having.

Yet her two-headed image was confusing some people more than she might have liked and it initially backfired. Rumour had it that the main reason Katy hadn't been kept on at Columbia was that executives were unsure of how to promote her. Could such a seemingly sweet and innocent girl really cut it as a sex kitten? Did she have the raw sex appeal that the average modern consumer expected to see on their TV screens? However, despite their apprehension, the contacts that she met at the label certainly hadn't forgotten her.

When Angelica Cob-Baehler, a senior publicist at the label, was frantically networking at the 2006 Grammy awards, she had nothing but good words to say about Katy. She believed her to be the new buzz-word, someone so new that she hadn't even arrived on planet Earth yet. By a sheer stroke of luck, Angelica then landed a job at Capitol Records working with veteran executive Jason Flom and his then junior A&R rep Chris Anokute.

Chris told *Hit Quarters*: "Angelica was telling us about this girl, Katy Perry, who was signed to Columbia. I said, 'Who's Katy Perry?' and she said, 'She's incredible. She used to be a Christian singer and Columbia doesn't really know what to do with her and they're about to drop her. I said, 'Well, send me the music!'"

Angelica sent him a three-track demo consisting of 'Simple' and two new tracks Katy had been working on, 'Thinking Of You' and 'Waking Up In Vegas'. Katy was beginning to take control of her own sound and so, unlike before, the impetus for these songs came from direct experience.

'Waking Up In Vegas' was about Katy's nights of decadence in the ultimate sin city. "Being from the greater Los Angeles area, Vegas is like a not-too-far-to-reach playground," she told *Tideline*. "It's one of those things – you're with some of your friends and you have some beer and you flip a coin and suddenly you're in Vegas."

She added, "Then you get there, and it's like, 'What the fuck, why do I feel this way?' You're like, 'Get me out of here!' So it's one of those things that everyone says, 'Yeah, we're gonna go and do this and do that and be crunk!' and the next morning you're like, 'Help me, I'm dying!'"

The song might have name-checked hangovers and hedonism but Katy's biggest inspiration was the fake marriage that had followed one of these nights, when she and her boyfriend had jokingly emulated Britney Spears' sham marriage at a tiny wedding chapel.

"I was 17 at the time," she recalled to *The Mail.* "My boyfriend and I were on a crazy weekend in Vegas and, on a whim, we decided it would be a fun idea to pretend to get married just to freak out friends and family. We bought a wedding dress and suit at a thrift store, picked up a wedding cake and went into the Little White Wedding Chapel to explain to the priest what we wanted. He seemed fine about it and even made up a fake wedding certificate. In the photos, our faces are saying, 'Why are we doing this crazy thing?' We sent the photos off to everyone we knew and they all completely freaked out. This whole stupid experience was the inspiration behind [the song]."

Some of her friends had hesitantly congratulated her, while others feared for her sanity, including her manager. Yet Katy's life wasn't all fun and games. When she had written 'Thinking Of You', it was not creating a hit single that she had in mind, but exorcising her frustration about the way life was treating her. Not only was she deep in depression due to the demise of her singing career, but she was also mourning the break-up of her relationship with Matt Thiessen. When the romance ended, Katy felt she had gone from a glamorous young woman living it up to a heartbroken nobody in a matter of weeks. This was the same person she had felt life would be worthless without. But instead of wallowing in self-pity, she wrote a song about it.

"That was a song I wrote in my apartment by myself and thought nothing of it," Katy later told *Blog Critics.* "It's not only my most personal song... but I really enjoy playing it. And when I play it, people are really moved by it."

Chris Anokute was one such person. To him, the demo had proved Katy could write both an upbeat singalong and a tender ballad – and he was sold. "I thought, 'This is a number one record!'" he revealed to *Hit Quarters.* "I took the demo and went to Jason Flom's office and said, 'Oh my God, I've found the next Avril Lavigne meets Alanis Morissette!' When I played him the demos, he wasn't sure if it was good enough.

More importantly, he had heard about her through the years and this wasn't the first time Katy Perry had been dropped. But because I was so passionate about it, Jason decided to come to a showcase."

The two watched Katy perform at both The Viper Room and The Polo Lounge, two major nightspots in LA. Jason certainly thought she had potential, but wasn't sure if he could make her successful in the increasingly cut-throat world of showbiz.

But Chris was persistent. He recalled, "I [was] so passionate about it that every single week I'm beating him up, trying to convince him to sign her, saying, 'Jason, we'll find the record, we'll develop her, we'll figure it out! There is something special about her – I know she is a star. Who cares that she was dropped?' We were determined to get this deal through...Almost seven weeks later, Jason emails me: 'It's great. What are we waiting for? Let's sign the girl.'"

It was the call that Katy had been waiting for, and it came during one of her shifts at the hated Taxi Music. "I got a phone call from the guy that ran Capitol Records because they were going to sign me and then decided not to sign me. That was my third record label to do that to me," Katy told *Seventeen*. "I was like, 'I'm not going through this again!' and he called me a few months later when I was sitting in that cubicle, and said, 'I'm sorry, I almost made the biggest mistake of my life in not signing you. I really believe in you! Let's just do it, let's just try!'"

Katy was incredulous. In this roller-coaster world, the only thing she'd become accustomed to was failure. But of all the things that had become consistent and familiar in her life, it was the one she would have the least grief kissing goodbye to. "I was like, 'Really?'" she recalled. "And he was like, 'Yeah, let's just try!' So we did it."

It was the perfect ending to a year of hell. Yet Katy would now be mentored by the team at Capitol for another arduous year. "We spent a year convincing people," Chris Anokute told *Hit Quarters*. "I even had her come to the office and no matter if it were interns, assistants, media people, sales people, I would just have her play acoustic guitar and showcase her songs to anyone who would listen. I had nine people standing around in my small office watching her play. This internal buzz-building was happening for a year."

Yet the fact that so many record-label employees remembered her had told Katy that her string of rejections wasn't down to a lack of talent, but merely bad timing.

"There were people that said, 'We've already spent money on her. We need fresh meat,'" Katy groaned to *CBS News*. "Everyone kind of looked at me a little bit like damaged goods, in a way. Like, you see a soup can in an aisle in a grocery store and it's kind of bent, you're not really going to buy that thing – although the soup inside it is probably still really delicious! There's no difference. It's gonna be a great bowl of soup! It took a wonderful group of people at Capitol to see beyond the dent and see that the dent was actually cool."

For Jason Flom, Katy's rejections eventually worked in her favour, proving that she was no quitter and was tenacious and serious about making it in the business. That set her aside from girls who sought stardom on a whim but bowed out when the going got tough. He was confident that she was in it for the long haul. "She spent several years working with many different producers only to find herself out on the street. Most people in her situation would have thrown in the towel, but true stars persevere," he mused.

Ironically, Katy later became such hot property that people were fighting over who had been the first to discover her. Jason Flom took exception to Chris Anokute's claims that he had been responsible for Katy's signing, insisting that while Chris was "definitely part of a wide-ranging team who all played valuable parts in Perry's breakthrough, he was not the primary driver of Katy being signed". He added that Chris had merely been an "energetic cheer-leader for the project".

The first step was to find a set of tunes to introduce her to the world, ones that would have modern music fans feverishly downloading the moment they heard them. Katy had written almost 70 songs since arriving in LA, but not all of them fitted the bill. 'Simple', for instance, quickly got cut.

Others were playful takes on the ups and downs of teenage relationships, such as the No Doubt-inspired 'My Boyfriend's Ex-Girlfriend', featuring the antics of a "psycho" girl who is unable to accept that her ex has moved on and is out for revenge.

However, although they liked the light-hearted melodies, Capitol sought more of a stand-out message for her launch pad into the wider music world, one that reflected who 22-year-old Katy was now. Some of her earlier tracks simply seemed too normal – and that was one thing Katy was not.

The plan was to release a combination of Capitol's favourites from the old tracks and the new ones they would work with her to pen in the studio. The songs spanned a five-year period, but the one theme that ran consistently through almost all of them was that they were pure pop. Unsure if this was her dream opportunity or merely another tantalising near-miss, Katy was nevertheless willing to take a chance and she signed on the dotted line.

Her CD was finally coming out, but the Katy that was being unleashed for the world to see was a million miles from where she'd started. It wasn't just talking sex that was a dramatic departure from the old days – it was also her musical style. Katy had once pledged to be the polar opposite of mainstream pop – but now it was all she could talk about.

Having shaken off her label as a harmless Christian gospel performer, she had then made a tentative foray into rock, attracted to the genre because it gave birth to an era of performers who spoke their minds and acted without regard for how others perceived them. Yet for Katy, when she started out, this lack of inhibition was an impossible dream. Flamboyant rock star show-offs struck a chord with the sheltered girl who'd had to conform to a Christian lifestyle for all of her existence, someone who was secretly sick of her every move being scrutinised. She didn't want to be forever judged according to God's law. These artists showed her that liberation was possible.

She also had a soft spot for the role of females in rock who, unlike their gospel counterparts, had a tough persona. Katy had been attracted to their devil-may-care attitudes and had loved being introduced to women like Shirley Manson of Garbage.

Consequently, much of her early work now featured a rock undertone – with the exception of her album with The Matrix – and it was what had made her feel the most comfortable. The track 'Rock God' had been written at just the right time, as its lyrics of dancing to a pounding rhythm and succumbing to a musical addiction was the perfect soundtrack to Katy's liberation.

She had come a long way, telling *The Telegraph*: "I get pissed off when singers don't take advantage of a good melody and a beat and put some kind of lyrics that make people feel something. It doesn't matter if it makes them want to dance or laugh or cry, or raises the hairs on their arms." Katy was all for responding to the powerful emotions that music aroused in her, whereas before she had related to the 10-year-old girl in *Jesus Camp*, who'd been scared to move to a beat for pleasure.

Christian music clearly hadn't suited Katy either, although she had insisted publicly that it was for God that she sang. "Yeah, you may have signed me to be a Christina Aguilera, but I'm doing this for me and God," she had told *Christian Music Central* defiantly. "I'm doing this because it's my time now. I didn't do this because you had some kind of idea that I would be somebody I'm not."

Perhaps this type of admission was what journalist Russ Breimeier had meant when he claimed that Katy "didn't endear herself to media". Yet, in spite of her clumsy delivery, she was still insisting that a Christian career, not a pop one, was what she had always wanted.

Ironically, some might say that Katy's story hadn't been much different from Christina's. Both had begun their public lives as demure teenagers who were attractive and alluring, but without flashing the flesh. They had sent out a message in no uncertain terms that they were not sex objects and that they were not available.

Christina was an elusive "genie in a bottle", someone who claimed her body might be telling her "yes" to sex, but her heart was saying "no". Her life had seemed to consist of chaste dates with chivalrous boyfriends, while Christina fluttered her eyelashes and played the role of a naive virgin. Yet the good-girl image was quickly eroded with the release of songs like 'Dirrty', which reinvented her as a promiscuous party girl out to satisfy her desires. She later claimed that the chaste image had never really been her, but more an invention of her record label.

Similarly, Katy had echoed Christina's message of refusing casual sex without commitment to begin with, but was now singing about one-night stands and, whether she had meant it in a musical or literal sense, selling sex. What was more, she was now doing so to a pop beat. She told *Black Book* of this period in her life: "I'm all about mainstream music. I'm not trying to hide anything. I'm trying to sell records. I've always wanted to do a big pop record and that's what I'm starting with."

She left no room for speculation or doubt when she spoke to *OMH* either, claiming: "I'm completely shameless! I love pop music. I've been around kids that hate selling records and enjoy being the starving artist. But I want to play stadiums. I want to sell records. I want to be a pop girl!" Yet, extraordinarily, just a few years earlier, Katy had shunned the genre altogether, claiming: "In the beginning I was doing pop, which was the complete antithesis of where I wanted to be."

Was Katy an instant fan of pop as soon as she had pushed aside her parents' warnings about music that lacked a religious agenda? Or had she sacrificed herself on the altar of conformity by choosing pop because she knew it was what the mainstream market wanted to hear?

Russ Breimeier told the author: "Katy could have tried again with another Christian label. She could also have gone independent or mainstream and still expressed her faith on her own terms or in subtle ways. But ultimately she chose instead to pursue mainstream music and a party lifestyle."

It seemed that Katy had run away from the expectations that were part and parcel of Christian music, that she was no longer content with playing the role. Like Christina, she was rebelling.

Forever a chameleon, she had now reinvented herself for the fourth time, in what some might say was a desperate last-ditch bid for success. If she failed this time, it could be back to Santa Barbara to work at a conventional job. Yet Katy's life revolved around music – she didn't have a university degree and she felt she'd come too far to end up doing the daily grind in an office. Even if Katy was branded an intolerable hypocrite, she didn't want to live a mundane life in suburban America – and perhaps she was prepared to do all she could to prevent that from becoming a reality.

Yet had Katy just abandoned God in her outward image, or had she internalised the change too? At 16, she had defiantly told *Cross Rhythms*, "I am who I am and I'm not really going to let anybody change me."

Yet in the months that had led up to the recording of the debut album, she had done a complete U-turn. Anyone who had told Katy pop was a good career move was now preaching to the converted.

Would the real Katy Perry please stand up? Who was she, for that matter? *CBS News* had wondered the same thing, asking her: "When you think back to your childhood in Santa Barbara going to church every weekend, being raised not being allowed to listen to the songs that you now sing, if I had told you back then that you were going to be this sexy pin-up pop star, would you have believed me?" With a smirk, Katy answered the feverishly debated question as to her real identity herself, replying: "I think it was always in the back of my mind that was the plan."

She added to *Star Scoop*: "Ultimately, I sold my soul to the devil."

Chapter 5

A Taste Of Cherry Chapstick

Katy now had a game plan – and it involved pure mainstream pop. While her Jesus tattoo might have comforted her in hours of darkness and appeased her anxious parents, it was not a good marriage with the career path she was about to follow. Her Bible was now discarded in a dusty corner, abandoned in favour of sex, drugs and rock 'n' roll.

The LA Times claimed: "Perry has Jesus tattooed on her wrist in fifties script, but she gets shy for the first and only time when it's pointed out, covering it with her band before reluctantly flashing it again." The tattoo now seemed little more than a dirty secret, one she wanted to obliterate completely from her public persona. Yet what that little tattoo represented to Katy was a reminder of God's forgiveness. For the part of her that still believed, she felt she was entitled to misbehave as much as she liked because she would always have her religious roots to fall back on. Misbehaving was inevitable now – just as her song had said, she'd chosen a path and she was following it, no matter what.

Katy's first flirtation with shock value came in the form of her debut single 'Ur So Gay'. The song outed her as a pop girl, venting her frustrations at falling in love with a man who wore more make-up than she did. It was a jibe at metrosexual men such as comedians Noel Fielding and Russell Brand and rock singer Brian Molko of Placebo.

The object of her affections was addicted to preening and examining himself in front of the mirror from every angle – this was someone who stole her clothes and owned more vanity products than she did – and Katy wasn't happy. How could she be the perfectly manicured princess when her man seemed prettier than she was?

After a long and bitter break-up, Katy was at her wit's end, so she decided to write a song. "It's about those guys that wear the guy-liner and use the flat irons and wear my jeans – I want to wear my jeans!" she told *Diva*. "It's about guys who spend more time in the mirror than their girlfriends do – and I wrote it after being dumped. It was one of those relationships where the dumpage lasted longer than the actual relationship, unfortunately, and I just remember after, finally, it was the last straw, kicking me out the apartment and not coming back. I went back to my house and I was a little upset."

Some girls might have comforted themselves with a box of tissues or a rant to their best friend. Yet Katy wasn't sobbing into her cornflakes after a sleepless night – instead, she found her revenge in the form of her lyrics. For someone who condoned being a bunny boiler, the terrified recipient of her anger might have expected voodoo dolls, pin cushions, dart boards adorned with his photo or even tweets denouncing the size of his tiny penis. Yet with the help of Katy's room-mate, a simple rhyme ended up cutting just as deep.

"I had this verse that I had been developing in my head and I played it to her and I was like, 'I don't know what to say in the chorus, he's just, like, so gay' and she's like, 'Say that'. I'm like, 'OK I'll say that!' It's taking the piss out of that emo scene."

The next person to hear Katy's creation was the man who had inspired it. "We had a conversation about it," she told *Metro Mix*. "We had some words. He was fine. I played him the song and said, 'C'mon, motherfucker, you're gonna dump me?' and he was like, 'Oh, shit.'"

To Katy, it was all fair play. Her disclaimer was that she'd already told the press how, when dumped, she would be prepared to "make your life hell". She chuckled to *The Telegraph*, "I'm sure there is some fine print at the bottom of my life which says, 'Warning – if you date her, you might have your genitals cut off in a song.'"

Her record company was keen for 'Ur So Gay' to be a taster single, available for free download from her website. They also wanted an arresting B-side to accompany it – and again, life experience dictated which one Katy would use.

"I go out dancing with my girls," she told *Prefix* magazine, "[and] 'Use Your Love', the original version by The Outfield, comes on and immediately every girl hits the dance floor. Everybody's out there dancing and trying to hit those notes." Katy wanted to capture that club vibe on her own CD and, after consulting her more music-savvy friends, she felt she'd found the perfect song.

"She wanted a song where no-one would be standing on the wall," an anonymous friend revealed. "She had in mind something that would make even the shyest girl get up and start dancing – and, hopefully, moving like she had a rocket up her ass. Over-the-top dancing that you see on Black-Eyed Peas' 'Time Of My Life' if need be. She wanted to have that crazy effect on people and 'Use Your Love' was the right song."

Next, she set about recording a video for 'Ur So Gay', which would be released on MySpace on November 20, 2007. The director was her friend Walter May. The budget was minuscule to nonexistent, but Katy's sense of humour came for free. She and Walter used Barbie-style dolls by Fashion Royalty as props, including a Ken figure with a perpetual desire to change his outfits, who played the gay character.

The video featured an angelic-looking Katy strumming on a guitar the colour of the Santa Barbara sea. The clouds above her had smiley faces, resembling a scene from *The Teletubbies*, and she was dressed in a demure polka dot top and a girlish hair bow.

If children's TV had sought to portray a teenage housewife from the forties, this was exactly how she might have looked. In fact, judging on appearance alone, Katy was the poster child for everything good, wholesome and pure. Yet vocally she was far from the spokeswoman for serenity and the lyrics told a different story. She graphically described strangling a troublesome ex with his H&M scarf and spoke with all the grace of a psychopathic mass murderer – yet she maintained an angelic, storybook smile all of the way through.

She was certainly subversive. Her anonymous friend confirmed: "You'd have to be deaf to think, 'Look at that nice Katy Perry!'" Indeed, Katy didn't want to be nice any more – the tune was her playground to be outspoken, ballsy and rock 'n' roll – all of the pleasures she'd been denied at home.

However, her desire to cause a stir backfired when she attracted fury from gay rights groups and the mass media. *Prefix* magazine stormed: "It seems that she would be heading right to the top of the charts – except, of course, for the fact that 'Ur So Gay', the song that she hopes will take her there, isn't so much a funny kiss-off as a juvenile bout of name-calling that borders on being offensive."

MSNBC agreed, adding: "If you substituted a different minority in Perry's tunes, they'd never get airplay. 'I Kissed A Black Guy' or 'Ur So Korean' would not be Top 40. For that matter, a song called 'I Kissed A Boy', sung by a guy, would probably die on the vine."

But perhaps the most plaintive response was from the pop culture site *After Ellen*. "You would never, not in a million years, see a major pop star launch into a revenge song called 'Ur So Asian' or 'Ur So Disabled'," it warned. "That would not and should not happen. But it is still somehow acceptable for an artist to sing a song like 'Ur So Gay' in revenge. We live in a country where gays and lesbians are still not allowed to openly serve their country in the military... We live in a world where LGBT youth are four times more likely to attempt suicide than their straight counterparts... a third of all LGBT youth have attempted suicide. And do you know where that all starts? Do you know what they've all been called? Do you know what you can hear today in any high school hallway? 'You're so gay!'"

Katy had unwittingly been swept into a political debate about gay rights and hostility was high – not the reception she might have hoped for when she was tentatively releasing her first ever pop single.

She was quick to defend herself, insisting to *The Times*: "The fact of the matter is that we live in a very metrosexual world. You know, a girl might walk into a bar, meet a boy and discover he's more manicured than she is and they can't figure it out. Is he wearing foundation and a bit of bronzer? But he's buying me drinks at the same time... I'm not saying,

'You're so gay, you're so lame.' I'm saying, 'You're so gay but I don't understand it because you don't like boys!'"

To Katy's mind, it was a jokey way of poking fun at someone who was technically metrosexual, but had almost certainly been gay "in another lifetime". She had been naively using the word "gay" like a playground buzz-word, perhaps not realising the negative connotations it might have had elsewhere.

What was more, in Katy's defence the song had been penned with and produced by Greg Wells, a writer who had also collaborated with the openly bisexual singer Mika. With this in mind, it seemed unlikely that the song had been anything more than a tease.

Katy told *The Telegraph*: "It's clear that not everybody's gonna hold hands and sing along like they would to 'We Are The World'. But some people look too deeply, like there is a conspiracy or an agenda with songs. Come on guys, I'm not out there to save the world – I'm just a pop singer!"

In fact, underneath the anger, there might even have been a glimmer of affection, if not recognition, for her ex's fastidious make-up routines. She clarified to *Buzznet*: "It's any guy who wears eye-liner and smudges it. It's just taking the piss out of this scene we call emo. There's a little emo in all of us."

However, not everyone saw it that way. Facebook groups emerged on the Internet in opposition to her with names like "Gay Guys Unite Against Katy Perry" and she received hate mail on her blog. "There have been people who don't know the premise behind it," she told *Metro Mix*. "They live to be offended and leave anonymous comments on my profile. I got a couple of people calling me a dumb bitch who should just throw herself in the river. But that's intense and I don't acknowledge it."

But was it more intense than lyrics that fantasised about strangling her boyfriend with his own scarf? Perhaps Katy had dug her own grave. Was the world cut out to understand her caustic sense of humour, let alone embrace it?

Things were not looking good for Katy. Corporate radio was unlikely to warm to a song that would offend both the homosexual and the homophobic population in equal measure. They might have been minority groups, but they were a force to be reckoned with. What had started out as a novelty song to raise a smile or a smirk from its audience had devolved into a widespread backlash.

It didn't help that in England at around the same time, an 18-year-old boy had been kicked to death for that very reason – being "too gay". This news made it a little harder for gay people to see Katy's song as purely a bit of fun. What was more, sales were extremely low. While the video had received over a million hits on MySpace, making it the second most popular video of all time on the site, that didn't equate to real-life sales.

Chris Anokute told *Hit Quarters*: "We didn't expect to sell 50,000 EPs and we sure didn't – we only sold a few thousand. In my opinion it did well in terms of building a press story, but because people didn't rush to iTunes to buy the EP, some executives in the record company started back-pedalling."

Although no-one had thought Katy would become an instant bestseller, expectations for the single had certainly been higher. Some felt she'd made her mark and could go on to greater things, yet others wondered if they had made a big mistake. As the murmurs of discontent got a little louder, the pressure rose. It was a testing time for Katy. If she failed, she could find herself on the scrap heap again, without a record label to release her material. An anonymous friend of Katy's revealed: "Katy might seem like a tough cookie and ordinarily she is, but it was her first proper single – can you imagine how it hurts when no-one has anything good to say about it? She was mortified, she just wanted to cringe."

Just when it seemed as though Katy might get dropped again, an unexpected ally came to her rescue – Madonna. Live on radio, she gave the thumbs up to the tune, declaring it her "favourite song of the moment".

To say that Katy was delighted would have been an understatement. "It was a huge moment for me," she told *Tideline*. "I broke out in hives. Yeah, I'm like, 'Madonna doesn't have time to listen to music, let alone know my first and last name, let ALONE be my cheer-leader!' Yeah, my dreams were definitely coming true."

Her dreams were also getting bigger – she began to tell the media that she wanted her own brand to be just as much a household brand as Madonna herself. While that might have been a little over-ambitious for an artist who'd barely broken the ice yet, Katy was determined to win the public over. Her message was validated by *Entertainment Weekly*, when it described 'Ur So Gay' as "eighteen shades of wrong". It might have sounded like a negative remark but, like Katy, it was an illusion. The journalist was in fact praising it, a song so wrong that it was right. Little by little, she was getting the positive press she'd hoped for.

But the struggle wasn't over yet – Katy still had to prove herself with her forthcoming lead single. If it wasn't a hit, there was still a chance she could be dropped. With her track record, no-one was more sensitive about the prospect of losing another contract than Katy.

She was also facing the opposition of her parents who, behind closed doors, were less than comfortable about the artistic company she'd been keeping. "I called my mom and said that Madonna went on the radio and said 'Ur So Gay' is one of her favourite songs," Katy enthused to *Metro Mix*. But she was bitterly disappointed by her mother's reaction. "It was negative, about how she sees Madonna's spread legs on every subway stop through Europe. That was her only reaction. But it's OK – I don't need to change them."

From that moment forward, it was up to Katy to stand alone against the world, sometimes facing both the highs and the lows by herself.

Anxious to get their hit single, Capitol teamed Katy up with top producer Dr. Luke, who had also worked with her when she was signed to Columbia. While her management had felt the Columbia recordings had lacked a distinctive, stand-out hit single, they were hoping that, this time around, they could change things.

Not the man to go to with a medical condition, Dr. Luke had nonetheless built up an excellent reputation for performing surgery on songs. The Polish-American writer had produced Avril Lavigne and Pink and would go on to work with names such as Ke$ha ('Tik Tok'), Jessie J ('Price Tag') and Britney Spears ('Hold It Against Me'). Not only did he have a track record for producing incredible hits, he also had an eccentric personality, fitting the profile of a mad professor rather than a doctor, so there would never be a dull moment in the studio. Believing that letting go of inhibitions was good for creativity, he encouraged artists to be violent on set, pepper-spraying him and stunning him with Taser guns.

Together, Luke and Katy recruited Max Martin, a king of cheesy but infectiously catchy pop. He was famous for his work with The Backstreet Boys, including smash hits 'Everybody' and 'I Want It That Way', and had also penned Britney's debut single as a 16-year-old schoolgirl, 'Hit Me Baby One More Time'.

Finally, equally talented ex-pop star Cathy Dennis was added to the mix. She had retired from a short-lived but successful pop career in the nineties to write behind the scenes and was responsible for 'Toxic', which Britney Spears described as her all-time favourite song of her career, and Kylie Minogue's 'Can't Get You Out Of My Head', a tune so contagious it had remained a club classic for years. Capitol felt that its songwriting team combined with Katy's voice and high work ethic would guarantee the label the hit single it was desperate to clinch.

Katy already had some ideas to bring to the table. She'd had a dream about a sapphic kiss 18 months earlier and now wanted to incorporate it into a song. "'I Kissed A Girl' was born as an idea in my head," she told *BBC News*." The chorus actually popped into my head when I woke up. It was one of those moments where you hear artists talking about songs they got in dreams or in the middle of the night."

Katy's song was about the "undeniable beauty" of women, focusing on an all-consuming crush she'd had as a teenager. "I was obsessed with her," she later told *Diva*. "I did everything she did. I couldn't believe that one person could be so delicate and flower-like and beautiful. She didn't even have to work at it. She'd wake up in the morning and she's just like a fawn. A little Bambi. She was always in the back of my head as that iconic beauty."

According to Katy, it was innocent curiosity rather than full-on lust that inspired her. She wasn't sure whether she wanted to be her crush or to be with her. But, either way, she was absolutely fascinated by her.

Katy grew to love the idea of the soft touch of women – their perfumed scent, their sensuous lips and their curvaceous figures – and she claimed it was sleepovers as a teenager that first awakened her curiosity. "You know, girls at a slumber party and they're hanging out with other girls," Katy told *The Times*. "We're all deathly afraid of that first kiss by that boy who we know is just gonna slobber all over our face." For that reason, she even wished that her first kiss had been with a girl.

Though quick to insist she was neither gay nor bisexual, and had a boyfriend, Katy wanted to write about the fluidity of sexuality. She was also thrilled to be working with Cathy Dennis, whom she claimed was "one of the best singers I've ever heard in my entire life. She has such a beautiful soft, sultry, sexy voice."

The song, recorded within the last two days of Katy's studio time, was an instant success with Chris Anokute, but there was some trepidation about whether the public would be offended by a counter-cultural song that spoke of kissing a girl and liking it.

"When she was cutting 'I Kissed A Girl', she comes into my office and plays me the song on her guitar," Chris recalled to *Hit Quarters*. "I thought, 'Oh my God, if the music is incredible, then this is a career record.' I couldn't wait to start playing it to people in the office, but for some reason people weren't getting it. One influential senior exec told me it sounded like an international club track. Other people said, 'This is never going to get played on the radio. How can we sell this? How's this going to be played in the Bible belt?'"

Overwhelmed by the opposition, Chris nevertheless continued to fight, feeling he knew better than the seniors he worked for. "I was 24," he recalled. "I know what young people out there listen to. I've partied and hung out socially with Katy and her friends and I know how she responded to music, so I kept on fighting. I convinced one of the radio guys to believe in the record. Dennis Reese saw the vision. So I had to use him to try to convince everyone to give this record a shot. So we have one shot. If this doesn't go, Katy is probably going to get dropped. We have to make a statement."

The pressure was on. Even Katy had her doubts, insisting to *Entertainment Weekly*: "When the label wanted to go with 'I Kissed A Girl', I was like, 'Nooo! I'm gonna come off like that's the only subject I know how to sing about!'"

But she was persuaded and, together with her cat Kitty Purry, she shot a video too. Katy was forced to overcome one of her most intense phobias for the recording – cat fur. "I have a problem with pet hair and lint," she explained. "Like, if I'm standing in line and a girl has a black cardigan on and she has pet hair all over the cardigan, I will leave or will just start picking like a monkey off her black cardigan and probably scare her. I'm so in love with my cat, but we have a love–hate relationship because I definitely have to walk out of the door every moment with a lint roller!"

A self-confessed OCD sufferer, Katy was terrified of fur clinging to her clothes – and not simply because it would be bad for her immaculate dress sense. According to statistics, OCD is especially common among the devoutly religious, and Katy had struggled many times with the impulse to shave her cat's fur off altogether.

However, she overcame her fears – stroking, cuddling and holding Kitty Purry close for the cameras with a blissfully untroubled grin on her face and no lint roller in sight. Her courage boded well for the single's release, which took place on May 17, 2008. Katy was on tenterhooks, telling *E! Entertainment*: "I knew this song was going to be the song that could possibly open all the doors. I knew it was just the kick-off."

Yet 13 years previously, a song by the same title had been banned from America's airwaves, so there was speculation about how radio stations would take to the track. This time around, the first station to add Katy's tune to their playlist was The River in the notoriously religious city of Nashville.

CEO Rich Davis told the author of his decision: "A record rep played it for me and I just remember it sounding like a big hit to me. I didn't get any complaints from anti-gay spokesmen, but I did get some feedback from moms who listen to my station who said that when it would come on the air, they would change the station. Once I got a few comments like that, I really had to weigh up whether playing it was worth it, since my job is attracting listeners. In the end, the song was a big hit and when Katy performed it on the *Today* show, I knew it had really reached mass appeal... it went on to become a number one record in the country.

AN ILL KATY FIGHTS BACK WAVES OF NAUSEA TO ROCK HER HELLO KITTY DRESS AND ACCEPT HER AWARD FOR BEST INTERNATIONAL FEMALE SOLO ARTIST AT THE 2009 BRIT AWARDS, HELD ON FEBRUARY 18 AT LONDON'S EARLS COURT. (MARK ALLAN/WIREIMAGE)

KATY LOOKS THE PART AT THE Q102 JUNGLE BALL AT CAMDEN, NEW JERSEY'S SUSQUEHANNA BANK CENTER ON DECEMBER 14, 2008, DRESSING UP AS A GLITTERY CHRISTMAS TREE FOR THE OCCASION. (BILL McCAY/WIREIMAGE)

SEXY SANTA: ANOTHER FESTIVE OUTFIT FOR KATY AS SHE PERFORMS AT THE 102.7 KISS FM JINGLE BALL AT ANAHEIM'S HONDA CENTER ON DECEMBER 6, 2008. THE DRESS WOULD BE WORN AGAIN THE FOLLOWING YEAR TO INTRODUCE HER PARENTS TO NEW LOVER RUSSELL BRAND. (JEFF KRAVITZ/FILM MAGIC)

BOY, GIRL OR UNDECIDED? IT'S A FREDDIE MERCURY MOUSTACHE AND SUIT ON THE LEFT AND A FLOWERY DRESS ON THE RIGHT, AS KATY POSES IN THE WINNER'S ROOM AT LIVERPOOL'S 2008 MTV EUROPE MUSIC AWARDS ON NOVEMBER 6. (GARETH CATTERMOLE/GETTY IMAGES)

KATY OVERINDULGES AT THE MTV LATIN AMERICA MUSIC AWARDS ON OCTOBER 16, 2008, IN GUADALAJARA, MEXICO, FALLING HEAD OVER HEELS INTO A GIANT PINK CAKE. (JEFF KRAVITZ/FILM MAGIC)

COVERED IN CAKE: KATY CONTINUES TO RAISE A SMILE AT THE MTV LATIN AMERICA AWARDS. (JEFF KRAVITZ/FILM MAGIC)

KATY ADDRESSES LIVERPOOL FROM HER BANANA-SHAPED THRONE AS SHE HOSTS THE 2008 MTV EUROPE MUSIC AWARDS ON NOVEMBER 6, 2008.
(KEVIN MAZUR/WIREIMAGE)

KATY STEPS OUT FOR THE 2010 MTV VIDEO MUSIC AWARDS AT LA'S NOKIA THEATRE ON SEPTEMBER 12, FLASHING THE FLESH IN A SHEER, BARELY THERE DRESS. (STEVE GRANITZ/WIREIMAGE)
INSET: KATY SHOWS OFF HER RUSSELL BRAND THEMED NAILS ON TWITTER. HER INDIGNANT EX-BOYFRIEND, TRAVIS MCCOY, LATER RAGED "IS THIS A JOKE?"

FEELING FRUITY: KATY PERFORMS AT LA'S 2009 GRAMMY AWARDS IN A FRUIT-ADORNED DRESS, ON FEBRUARY 9. (KEVIN MAZUR/WIREIMAGE)

Could the track have been perceived as being on the edge? Sure, but it must not have been too controversial to have achieved that kind of success."

Despite the song's popularity, there were two major groups that opposed it. First there were the strictly religious members of society who believed the Bible taught that homosexuality was a sin. Then there was the gay community, who were furious with Katy for trivialising a gay lifestyle and seemingly using it to stir up sensation and add to her record sales. A steadily growing third group merely thought that Katy was a fake, regardless of any political connotations.

The Times was one such newspaper, insisting: "The Russian pop duo t.A.T.u exploited lesbianism much more saucily than Perry." Tatu was a pair of teenage girls who claimed to love each other and filmed a passionate on-screen kiss for the promotional video of their first single, 'All The Things She Said'. According to some reports, they quickly became the most hated teenagers in Russia, while the less conservative Brits found their relationship – complete with kissing live at shows – a turn-on. The illusion of lesbian love was somehow shattered when one of the girls got pregnant, after which they disappeared from the charts altogether. It sparked criticism that their popularity was based on their stage antics and shock value alone.

Tatu's manager Ivan Shapovalov, the Russian equivalent of Simon Cowell, later claimed that one of the girls had bedded him for a chance of stardom, that he'd wanted to manufacture another shock-value song called 'Daddy, Don't Touch Me There' and that he was obsessed with marketing groups on their personal lives. Finally, he encouraged the girls to sing in English, despite not understanding a word of the language when they recorded their single. It was widely assumed that both acts were fake, but Katy's video was criticised for failing to be as daring as Tatu and not featuring an on-screen kiss.

Katy had an answer for that accusation. "I didn't want to be so literal," she told *Diva*. "This isn't your freak show of girls making out. Some people still have a problem with it, but there's much more crazy, raunchy stuff on MTV – I mean, have you ever seen a hip-hop video?! My perspective is a little bit tongue-in-cheek, cute, flirtatious, curious.

A little Betty Boop here and there... It walks a line of provocative. But I've seen people fucking hop off the line and jump in the pool!"

Katy certainly knew where to stop. She'd had enough practice of walking a fine line in her staunchly religious childhood. While a suggestion of kissing a girl was a risqué head turner, a song claiming "I kissed my Great Dane and I liked it" would have been downright offensive. She knew exactly how far to go without being trapped by the censors – and she'd turned gentle provocation into a fine art.

However her comments horrified some gay activists. Not only was she depicting a gay kiss as a potential "freak-show parade", she also insisted "when we're young, we're very touchy-feely... it's not perverse, but just sweet". Was Katy saying that lesbian love affairs were perverse and that so-called innocent experimentation was as far as a good girl could take it?

The line "It's not what good girls do" demeaned the gay community, but to Katy it was a simple, honest recollection of how lesbian longings had affected her personally, having been raised in an environment where it was unacceptable to feel those things. "I understand where people who experience prejudice are coming from – I've grown up around a lot of ignorance," she explained to *Diva*.

She added to *The Advocate*: "I guess it is a subject that is close to my heart. I have a lot of friends who are gay and I have kissed a girl. I grew up in a very strict environment where that was considered what you call an abomination – and I fucking hate that word!"

However, famous lesbian Beth Ditto of the rock group The Gossip, was not pacified by Katy's explanations. "I hate Katy Perry!" she announced to the gay magazine *Attitude*. "She's offensive to gay culture. I'm so offended! 'I Kissed A Girl' is a boner dyke anthem for straight girls who like to turn guys on by making out or, like, pretending to be gay. She's just riding on the back of culture without having to pay any of the dues and not being lesbian or anything at all."

When Katy was quizzed by *The London Paper* on Beth's rant, she responded diplomatically, insisting: "I don't want to get into a slanging match with anybody so I don't want to say anything bad about her – but I'm not impressed. I've learned in the past year that one artist should never insult another artist's music – it's tacky."

Ironically, Beth had previously voiced negative words about gay culture, claiming that skinny, dangerously thin catwalk models were the fault of gay men who imposed their own desires of androgyny on the fashion industry. She felt that they repressed the display of women's natural curves. "If there's anyone to blame for size zero, it's not women," she said. "Blame gay men who work in the fashion industry and want these women as dolls."

When she heard that Katy wasn't impressed, she spoke out again, this time matching her diplomacy. "It's not about Katy Perry," she told *Star Pulse*. "It's about this song and it's innocence on her part. To Katy, it's just this party song. But as a gay person, it's like, 'Oh, of course, this straight person singing about kissing a girl goes straight to Top 40 and people buy this record. Who can give a fuck about real gay people?' That's what's really painful about the whole thing."

She added: "It's like, 'Oh, that's what you think? Of course, because you never thought about what a real gay person feels and the impact that a song like that has on the gay world in a time of crucial civil rights.'"

She blamed Katy's song for reducing lesbian sexual orientation to an act for male entertainment. She also highlighted the gay rights issue by telling of a time when she was having major surgery and was unable to have her female partner by her side. "You try being a really scared 23-year-old in this hospital room that's 3,000 miles from home and the only person that you have is your partner, who can't stay because you're not married or they're not your relative. That's insane and absolutely scares me to death," she continued.

Giving Katy a final piece of advice, she insisted: "I don't care if she writes a song about kissing a girl, but there are people who kiss girls in their everyday life and it's not as easy as just kissing a girl and everyone loving you. It would be really rad to hear her talk about something like that."

Katy tried to brush off the "intense" comments her song had garnered by claiming it had been a light-hearted "joke" all along, but this only increased lesbian campaigners' fury. In the video for the single, Katy's curiosity is merely a brief dream after which she wakes up with a man by her side to resume her ordinary heterosexual life – her gay desires little more than a figment of her imagination. Critics might say they had never existed.

Even *The Times* ultimately accused Katy of yawn-worthy part-time lesbianism, writing: "Perry is careful to insist that this is just a bit of lesbian tourism... in the end [she] opts for heterosexuality and skulks away from full-time lesbianism. Still, it has generated some star-making controversy for her."

That was another facet of the song that caused criticism for Katy. Even magazines accused her of deliberately faking lesbianism both to become a sex symbol to men and to sell more CDs. *Slant* magazine claimed: "'I Kissed A Girl' isn't problematic because it promotes homosexuality, but because its appropriation of the gay lifestyle exists for the sole purpose of garnering attention, both from Perry's boyfriend and the audience."

Meanwhile *AllMusic* wrote: "The problem is not with Katy's gender-bending, it's that her heart isn't in it. She's just using it to get her places, so she sinks to crass, craven depths that turn [her songs] into a grotesque emblem of all the wretched excesses of this decade."

Finally *Digital Spy* delivered the most cutting review, claiming: "It's nothing that Gwen Stefani, Girls Aloud or even Britney Spears on a good day couldn't have handled with more aplomb... the lyrical content is about as saucy as a seaside postcard from 1974 — all nudges and winks rather than anything truly groundbreaking or controversial. It's an enjoyable enough three minutes but it's hard to see the record as anything other than a cynical marketing ploy that's cashing in on male adolescent fantasies with its almost raunchy video."

However, Katy had never denied that the theme of the song was a marketing ploy. "Some people are fascinated with the idea of a great storyline: good girl, Christian parents, goes bad," she told *Q* magazine. "'I Kissed A Girl' provided the perfect storyline, so it's entertaining for people."

Using life experiences for entertainment was exactly what the gay community loathed and the straight community mocked about Katy. Some felt they'd been taken for a ride. Whether or not she had harboured desires for other women, the story was manufactured for maximum publicity.

Perhaps she wasn't as innocent as she looked. She told *Blog Critics* of her persona, "I'm obsessed with how Lolita can straddle the line of being sweet and innocent, but she knows exactly what she's doing, y'know? I see a lot of myself like that." Indeed, while Katy might act coy and unassuming, she knew exactly how to market herself and what effect it might have.

Next, Katy was jokingly accused of plagiarism by Jill Sobule, a lesbian pop star from the nineties. She had been managed by the same person who was now masterminding Katy's career, Jason Flom, and she felt that it was a little more than coincidence that Katy was singing a tune with the same title as her own effort, released in 1995.

She told lifestyle and culture magazine *The Rumpus*: "As a musician, I have always refrained from criticising another artist... it did bug me a little bit, however, when she said she came up with the idea for the title in a dream. In reality, she wrote it with a team of professional writers and was signed by the same guy that signed me in 1995. I have not mentioned that in interviews as I don't want to sound jealous or petty, because that's not me."

She then had a change of heart, continuing: "OK, maybe if I really think about it, there were a few jealous and pissed off moments. So here goes, for the first time in an interview – fuck you, Katy Perry, a fucking stupid, maybe 'not good for the gays' title-thieving, haven't heard much else, so not quite sure if you're talented, fucking little slut."

Jill had intended the comments as a joke, but she was misinterpreted and was soon inundated with hundreds of emails and Facebook messages from furious Katy supporters. One such message asked, "HOW DARE YOU? Calling Katy Perry a slut. I'm so pissed at you right now. So are the rest of her fans. Why did you do that?"

To try to right the wrong, Jill told *The Huffington Post* of the online interview: "I prefaced my reply with a wink and then rambled on with a string of over-the-top dumb-ass profanities, purposely out of character and completely in jest... a few weeks later, the quote was picked up in the tabloids out of context and without that – hard to sometimes see in print – wink... I have never really been angry or had ill feelings towards Katy herself. That said, I hope her and her fans – God knows I don't want to piss them off any more – are OK with the title of my brand new song, 'I Kissed A Girl... First.'"

In fact, the spat – with Jill's witticisms included – only served to create more publicity for them both. Joking aside however, Jill did have some reservations about the authenticity of the song. She felt that her song was a genuine anthem for lesbian women and at the time boundary-breaking, whereas Katy's was not.

She told the author: "This was 1995 and there was no song of its kind. It was really taboo. The USA has some religious rights nutters. Anyway, I first wrote it on a lark, not thinking it would ever see the light of day. At the same time, I did want to write a lesbian or bisexual-themed song – something that I wish I could have heard when I was a sexually confused teen. I wanted to sing an affirming, empowering anthem. I think by using humour, I was able to pass the censors."

She felt that her own message, that of a tortured young woman trying to come to terms with her unconventional sexuality, was more positive than Katy's. "I thought [her song] trivialised sexuality," she claimed. "It was more 'Spring Break Girls Go Wild' or 'I'll kiss a girl to tease my boyfriend and sell records' than a true queer song. To this day, I get women who come up to me and say my song helped them come out or not feel so alone and monstrous when they were young. If there are young girls who feel the same way about Katy's version, then more power to her."

Jill was perhaps frustrated, however, that her song had been banned on a number of radio stations for obscenity – and therefore failed to achieve the success she'd been hoping for – while Katy's version had been universally accepted on air. Besides that, she felt her management team had manufactured the theme of the song based on their work with her.

"Her A&R man, Jason Flom, was also mine during her 'I Kissed A Girl' period," she explained. "I'm sure he felt he could repeat the success. And boy did they! Way more than mine."

She added controversially: "Katy wrote that song with a team of pro writers. I'm not sure if it was her or the other writers' idea, [but] I had a hard time thinking that her team had not heard of my song."

Katy now faced charges of insulting lesbians and pretending to kiss girls purely to sell her product. There was even doubt over the originality of her song. Yet the harshest criticism of all came from the church-going community.

"I was disappointed by the trashy lyrical content," Russ Breimeier told the author. "Her lyrics sometimes have a bratty quality to them... it's as if she'd say or do anything for attention. For me, the biggest problem with Katy's lyrics and persona over the years is that they've become too provocative. The Bible has strong words for those who would lead others to sin, and that includes flaunting our sexuality. Whether or not Katy intended the song as a joke, a lot of people take offence to it. Taken at face value, it's a song about sexual exploration in light of losing control i.e. getting drunk. So yes, I think that contradicts what Christians are taught according to the Bible."

Russ wasn't the only one to be confused. Katy had pledged to her religious fans in *Christianity Today*: "I just want to be real. I'll never wear a mask." Yet readers were now wondering who the real Katy was – the God-fearing girl whose values they'd always admired, or the brash sex kitten who'd written an anthem for lipstick lesbianism?

Journalist DeWayne Hamby, who had instantly loved Katy when he'd interviewed her as a teenager, was one of the listeners who wasn't quite so sure. "When she hit mainstream, I was torn in my feelings in that I was proud she was having success, but sad that the gospel music industry lost such a promising talent," he told the author. "I also hated that a voice like hers that could have continued to provide encouragement to Christian teens trying to live counter-culturally had now become a voice of the culture they're trying to escape."

He added: "I like that she doesn't seem to take herself too seriously, but I don't like how she keeps referring to herself as a rebellious preacher's girl, because I think that's a little gimmicky and it's a pet peeve of mine to trumpet your rebelliousness like that. Also, I'm disappointed that we have another female singer who relies on sexuality to get attention."

The song was banned altogether in Singapore and there was no ambiguity in Haven's Corner evangelical church in Ohio, which signposted its gardens with the phrase "I kissed a girl and I liked it, so I went to hell!"

Katy's fans denounced the slogan for being judgemental, suggesting that people should be free to make their own decisions, as each individual would be held responsible for themselves alone on Judgement Day. As for Katy herself, she passionately believed that the afterlife was not as simple as Heaven or Hell.

Yet the song continued to offend as far afield as Brazil, where a teacher was sacked for giving teenagers the lyrics to study in one of his classes. The head teacher believed that the song promoted alcohol abuse and homosexuality.

Christian websites pulled together in an attempt to "save Katy's soul". One such site could barely disguise its fury. "Katy is promoting and glorifying the vile sin of homosexuality!" it raged. It listed the "filthy, un-Christian, shameful" lyrics before arguing: "Katy Perry is a disgrace to her parents, Christianity and America. Certainly, Katy Perry is not honouring her parents as the Bible commands, when she sings songs promoting lesbianism. Is this honouring to Jesus Christ? No, absolutely not! Homosexuality is an abomination to God."

It continued: "Katy Perry is of the devil. Satan is a beautiful liar. Don't be deceived by the beauty of the devil's music – rock and roll is straight from Hell and will corrupt your morals. First came rock and roll, then fornication, then came abortion and now homosexuality. Next will be outright idolatry and Luciferian worship."

The website even denounced her entire family for speaking in tongues, claiming that it was not a spiritual activity, but a form of "witch-craft". Bewildered by the negative responses, Katy had no choice but to step in and defend herself. Perpetually labelled the preacher's daughter, she tried to explain that she was no more a spokesperson for religious righteousness than she was a political activist. "My platform in life isn't necessarily to preach," she told *The Advocate*. "I respect everybody's faith. For me, honestly, it took a while to get to that point of respecting everybody's opinion. I was raised in a household where that wasn't necessarily allowed. There's no such thing as respecting everybody's faith in my kind of upbringing."

Although she was publicly outing her parents as extremists, she hadn't nearly finished yet. "I'm in the business of rock 'n' roll," she argued. "I make mistakes. I'm human. I'm flawed. I accept that. I'm not here to preach the Gospel right now other than to be a good fucking musician."

She continued: "First of all, the song is about an obvious curiosity. It's not about anything intense. The fact of the matter is that girls, a lot of the time, smell much better than boys. We smell like vanilla. We smell like watermelon. We smell like strawberries. So, duh! One day I was out with my boyfriend and I opened up a magazine and realised, 'You know what, honey? I would probably make out with Angelina Jolie if she wanted to.' The song is about the beauty of a woman and how that's changed a lot of things in life. It's started wars. It's ended wars. In general, it doesn't matter if you're female or male, if the right woman walks through the door, everybody's jaw is going to be on the floor."

Katy was growing up quickly under the glare of the media spotlight. Things that she'd been denied access to all of her life – fashion, magazines, TV, music, a secular lifestyle – were now right under her nose and she was sharing the excitement of those joyful first experiences with the public. That was what was so appealing about Katy to her fans, what made her stand out. Many girls would have lost the first-time thrill of an activity years earlier and become blasé. Yet five years previously, Katy wouldn't even have had access to a glossy magazine to take lustful glances at Angelina Jolie.

However, while she couldn't wait to share her sexual awakening with the world, not everyone reciprocated her feelings. Despite the insistence that the song was light-hearted, no-one was more horrified about her departure from Biblical teachings than Katy's parents.

The Daily Mail claimed her mother had launched a "ferocious attack" on Katy, saying: "I hate the song. It clearly promotes homosexuality and its message is shameful and disgusting... I can't even listen to that song... when it comes on the radio, I bow my head and pray." She allegedly also claimed that her daughter had been led astray by her party-loving Hollywood friends. However, Katy laughed off the accusations, insisting: "I don't know whose mom they spoke to, but it certainly wasn't mine."

Perhaps the media was playing a practical joke on Katy. However, at a sermon they led at the Legacy Church in Springfield, the family made their true feelings clear. Reverend Darren Hearnsberger introduced them with the speech: "The overall message here is that we may stray, but God still loves us. No matter how terrible our lives get, we can never outrun the love of God."

Katy appreciated the gesture, telling *The Daily Telegraph*: "I have my own beliefs and they would certainly be different to how I was raised. But when it comes to my family, we agree to disagree and we're OK with that. To the day they die, I'm sure my parents will be praying for me and my salvation. I respect that and I'm happy they do."

Salvation was certainly on the mind of her father, Keith, who told the congregation: "I can't just look at Katy Perry who is my daughter. I've got to see her for what God sees her for. I can't just see her because she is big and famous. I've got to say, 'God, what do you see?'... I love her, we have a wonderful relationship, although I'm not excited about everything she does. When she wrote the song 'I Kissed A Girl', I said, 'Oh my God! I kissed God and I liked it better!'"

Tensions were still running high when a message appeared on the website *Beliefnet*, allegedly posted by Katy's parents, claiming that her soul needed to be saved. "The issue is salvation," it read. "Our hearts yearn for the restoration of people like Katy. We witness to Katy as much as we can, however when people are in darkness, the light hurts their eyes... [but] there is light at the end of the tunnel."

While they stopped short of calling her a Judas, whose actions had betrayed Jesus, others weren't so restrained. A blogger for *Today's Christian* claimed icily: "It seems that Katy has lost sight of the importance of God in her life and decided to throw out a struggling Gospel career for some cold, hard cash. Another person comes to mind right away for me here and that's Judas. Judas was a sell-out."

Christian journalist John J Thompson had equally strong words, implying that her music should be boycotted. "I do not believe an artist needs to be singing about Jesus all the time to be appropriate for Christian audiences," he told the author, "but I know flat-out heathens who won't let their kids listen to her! Her image and persona are completely contrary to any Biblical example as far as I can see and I have not heard anything from her that would lead me to believe she thinks about life through a prism of faith, grace or holiness."

However, as a growing number of Christian followers, including some who had previously purchased her album, stepped out to criticise her, Adam LaClave of the Christian group Earthsuit disagreed, telling the author: "As fellow human beings, not Gods, we shouldn't be in the game of auditing each other's values by the things we think we can see. Some people's lives are so mundane that they like to project their self-disappointment or jealousy onto other people under the guise of concern. I know that Katy's fan base has made a sport out of doing that with her, and I'm sure it annoys the hell out of her as it has me ever since I left the bubble ten years ago. That said, I think Katy Perry is actually very similar to Katy Hudson in personality – she's just selling her goods to a different demographic now."

That new demographic would prove to be far more accepting of Katy. While *The Observer* had argued: "You're not a sassy liberated woman exploring your sexuality, you're pandering to the oldest image in male porn – and there's nothing daring about that", *The Chicago Sun-Times* challenged: "The fact that our society is beginning to accept that there isn't always one box (gay or straight) for people to check is a good thing."

Some feared it portrayed lesbian love as a fulfilment of male fantasies rather than a desire in its own right, implying it existed only as a mere teaser and a prelude to conventional boy-girl sex. Others felt differently. Even if Katy was considering purely her sales when she sang it, the song was still forcing an uncomfortable taboo out in the open, normalising same-sex flirtation in society and potentially making gay women feel less isolated.

The Jill Sobule track of the same name had been banned from some radio stations for being provocative, so surely the title's appearance on radio now proved just how far gay rights had come. Also, mainstream artists had never released two songs in a row about alternative sexuality and retained popularity before. Perhaps Katy was about to change preconceptions about homosexuality in America forever.

"The song is a valid expression of desire that appeals to many women, irrespective of their sexuality," claimed Louise Carolin, editor of the lesbian magazine *Diva*. "It annoys me when straight men assume those girl-on-girl snogs are all for them and I think it's a pity when lesbians make the same assumption." Her support was a surprise, as not all of the gay community had been so welcoming.

It was a big consolation to Katy after the backlash when her single became an overwhelming commercial success. It went platinum in 13 countries, topped charts in more than 20 and ultimately sold over six million copies worldwide. A month after its release, the song reached the top spot on America's Hot 100 *Billboard* chart, where it remained for seven weeks running. In Britain, meanwhile, it remained at number one for five weeks in total, before losing out to Kings of Leon's 'Sex On Fire'. Katy achieved the highest chart position for a debut artist in over five years – and to think this was a tune the record label was concerned would never get played in the Bible belt!

In typical rock 'n' roll style, Katy couldn't even remember where she was when she made it to number one. But when she heard the news, she was living up to her stereotype and partying. "I don't remember the specific city but I knew we [soon] had a day off in Las Vegas, which was exciting because that is the best place to celebrate anything, right? My producer sent me a bottle of Dom Perignon and it showed up at the hotel. We took it and sat by the pool. We just raised our glasses and said, 'How the hell did we do this?'"

With her plentiful supply of alcohol, Katy had just committed another abomination – but it seemed unlikely that she would care.

The song had even knocked Lady Gaga off her pedestal. Talking of her smash hit 'Just Dance', Gaga told *The Guardian*: "It just doesn't sound like Katy Perry's 'I Kissed A Girl'. It's a beautiful, lovely, amazing hit record and it sounds like a radio hit – but my song doesn't sound like a radio hit."

How wrong she was – yet it seemed that, just for a moment, Katy had made the world's new queen of pop a little insecure.

The song also attracted the attention of Katy's ultimate crush, the actress Scarlett Johansson. Katy had been telling the media that she would happily lock lips with her, claiming, "She's beautiful. She's such a lady too. She reminds me of a pin-up girl." She added "She's my girl crush… she is a very classy young lady and she knows how to walk the line of being a sex kitten and a young woman."

Scarlett responded by telling *Allure*: "That's flattering, but my lips are kind of taken." She was also after royalties, joking, "I should get a cut!"

Katy might not have kissed Scarlett – in fact, she'd publicly been turned down in favour of her then husband, Ryan Reynolds – but she'd cheated failure and forced her way to a place in the charts, and she was thrilled.

What was more, even some devoutly religious spokespeople had come around to her way of thinking. "Underneath all the boundary-pushing and edginess is a girl who still loves Jesus," Mark Moring of *Christianity Today* told the author: "I don't think musicians are obliged to sing about God all the time. I think they should be free to write and sing songs about real life."

Meanwhile Matthew Turner, whose blog expressed that Christians should love one another irrespective of sexuality joined in singing her praises. He believed that the conflict between the two sides of Katy made her realistic and relatable and was part of her appeal. "The most beautiful part about Katy's story is her journey towards being completely real, authentic, honest. Every religious person has a wild side, but only the honest people ever allow that side to be revealed."

Finally, Philip Von Wrede, the sales rep for her Christian record company, told the author, "At the end of the day Katy was expressing herself without limiting herself to the thoughts of what others may think of her. I'm glad she took a gamble at being outrageous and glad it paid off. From a Christian level, I think God invented us to be creative and honest, regardless of how unorthodox it may be at times. When she debuted with 'I Kissed A Girl', my first thoughts were, 'I'm sure this isn't going down too well with her parents!' My second thought was that the single was going to build positive controversy in the way that 'Like A Virgin' by Madonna got kids talking in the early eighties." That would have been music to Katy's ears and proof that the chorus was working.

He concluded: "My overall thoughts were, 'That's right, Katy, come out with your guns blazing! Be yourself and let the sun shine on those cherry chapstick lips!'"

Chapter 6

Underneath The Candy Coating

Katy did just that, touring the country armed with a giant inflatable chapstick. She also increased the dose of her trademark honesty by releasing her opinionated new album, *One Of The Boys*.

It hit the shops on June 17, 2008 and showcased her biggest trademark of all, her acid tongue. On her hit list were men who are too archetypally feminine ('Ur So Gay'), too archetypally masculine ('Mannequin'), too penny-pinching ('If You Can Afford Me') and too indecisive and emotionally challenged ('Hot And Cold'). In fact, any man who had ever wronged her was publicly humiliated by becoming the talking point in a song.

However, beneath the caustic taunts, Katy also revealed a hidden side to herself. She might have seemed career-focused and competitive, but her ultimate ambition was to find love. "One of life's ultimate mysteries [is] the communication between men and women," Katy told *Digital Spy*. "We're all in the hustle of life to find love!"

Perhaps she was growing into a woman after all – not just one of the boys. That was the theme of the album's self-titled first track – as Katy awakens sexually, she changes from the girl who was every boy's burping partner, realising that her "down with the dudes" attitude is not erotic. In her childhood she would have jumped off a roof for kicks, was happy to get muddy on the football field and would never have turned down a dare.

However, she now sought not to be the daredevil who was the centre of everyone's attention, but the mysterious, alluring object of their desires. Striking a balance between femininity and friendship with the boys would become a theme of the young Katy's life. "Some people say, 'Katy, you're one of the boys, but you still keep your red lipstick intact,'" she told *Tideline*. "If I need to kick off my heels and play kickball, trust me, I will."

She continued: "It's a coming of age song [about] that summer between junior high and high school when all the girls suddenly grew and changed from being someone guys made fun of to being this Bambi-like creature that they wanted to be with. The girls grew, changed, developed and all of a sudden the boys stopped trying to make fun of them and started wanting to be around the girls... because they looked pretty and smelled pretty."

While Katy wrote the song independently on her guitar, the next track, 'I Kissed A Girl', was transformed by a team of professional writers. Following its success, co-writer Cathy Dennis praised: "It feels to me like a real song of the moment. It's a bit controversial and makes people think, which is a good thing. Katy Perry is original, the video is funny and engaging and, although it's always a bit of a shock to hear that you have a number one record in the States and that you've sold a million downloads, I always felt that the blend of the song and the artist was so strong that we stood a good chance of having a hit!"

'Waking Up In Vegas' was another infectiously catchy potential hit. However, while Cathy had been the queen of pop, this song was produced with Desmond Child, who added a rock element. He had previously written for Joan Jett, Bon Jovi, Aerosmith and Kiss ('Crazy Nights'). He stepped outside of his comfort zone of anthemic rock tunes to give Katy a soft, rich flavour with a belting chorus.

Another producer, Andreas Carlsson, joined them in the studio to channel the experience of living it up in sin city. He told *Hit Quarters*: "We really wanted to tell the story that described that moment when everybody's checking out of Vegas after they've had their fun – and Katy is the perfect artist to tell a story. She has humour and knows how to deliver it... I already had the guitar riff of the song. The phrase 'put your money where your mouth is' was something that we always wanted to use – it was almost the title but ended up in the chorus. I don't know where that Vegas thing came from, but I was a big Elvis fan and it just seemed right at the time."

'Thinking Of You' had a darker, more melancholic side and was first penned by a desperate and penniless Katy on her acoustic guitar. It told of the struggles she had in moving on after reluctantly ending a love affair. "It's probably the best representation of me [on the album] because I wrote it myself," Katy told *Alloy*. "It's a song that I think resonates in a lot of people's personal lives. It was a song I wrote being in a relationship and having to move on, not really necessarily wanting to move on in that relationship, but thinking I had to and then finding myself with other people and hanging out with them, and feeling a really guilty feeling of cheating or something."

Sandwiched together on the album are 'Mannequin' and 'Ur So Gay'. Katy can't decide whether to berate her boyfriend from being an over-sensitive metrosexual or to denounce him for seeming not to feel at all. When he is wearing guy-liner, perfecting his emo poses and borrowing her jeans, she baulks. However, when the same person reverts to masculinity, she's still not happy, claiming she wishes he could feel instead of behaving like a mannequin.

"I was in a relationship where the other person was nonexistent," she told *Monsters And Critics*. "They were totally having mannequin characteristics. Like, all I wanted to do was love and be loved in return. It just wasn't happening. I think it was just because of personal problems, things that they were going through. I did not get through to them for some reason. I tried everything."

Meanwhile Katy lamented to *The New Gay* magazine that she always ended up dating men who were "very sensitive, good-looking and smell good". Some women would have been delighted, but for Katy this simply signalled that her man's self-interest was becoming greater than his interest in her.

One consistent theme that runs through both songs, however, is Katy's longing for attention and affection and her frustration when she feels she receives less than she deserves. Did the man in question neglect her or was she simply more high-maintenance than he could handle?

Katy's demands continue in 'If You Can Afford Me', where she tells a hopeful admirer that she "doesn't put out for charity". She told *Metro Mix*: "That's about a girl being sassy to a guy – 'It takes more than a wink, more than a drink.' It's a weird thing, dating these days. In Hollywood, a guy asks a girl to go to dinner and thinks he's going to get something out of it. So the song is a message that says, 'Please, I'm worth more than that.'"

Yet Katy seems to imply that, if the price is right, she's game for more. Katy had displayed an obsession with wealth and power from the beginning, christening her ASCAP publishing name 'When I'm Rich, You'll Be My Bitch'.

Here, she was using her sex appeal to be powerful. Some saw her as a cold-hearted, calculating woman dead set on getting what she wanted and willing to turn romance into a transaction. The song offended feminists and male suitors alike, with *NME* denouncing it as a "sexless 'Bills Bills Bills'".

Destiny's Child had been one of Katy's first secular musical experiences after leaving home, seeing her develop a passion for the song 'Bug A Boo', so perhaps 'Bills Bills Bills' had been an inspiration, although the latter criticises men for asking their female lovers to pay the bills.

Those who heard Katy's version might have wondered whether she was a smart, sassy girl out for herself and self-respecting enough not to give away her body – or merely a prostitute. However, she later concedes in the lyrics: "I don't need your dollar bills." The song had the potential to be both as controversial and as misunderstood as 'Bills Bills Bills' – and perhaps that was exactly Katy's intention.

On 'Hot And Cold', she returns to dissecting male motivations. According to an anonymous church-goer, Katy's mother had said that the song was based on a Biblical reference. She explained: "I listened to her mother, Mary Hudson, speak at my church in Kalamazoo, Missouri, and she loves her daughter very much and of course is not pleased with her songs now, but knows that she will come back to the Lord, who she was raised with all her life. In fact, the song 'Hot And Cold' refers to a passage from the Bible that says you are either hot for God or cold. This is something that Katy grew up hearing from her parents when they were teaching her the word of the Lord. It won't be long, Katy will be on fire for God again and still singing, but this time singing for God!"

However Katy had a different explanation. "It's about a relationship," she told *Digital Spy*. "I was with this boy I really, really cared for and we'd be having a conversation by text or by email and then he'd just disappear, for like three days. It would drive me crazy cos I would be like, 'I thought we were making plans for this weekend?' I realised that this guy was the moodiest motherfucker I ever met and honestly that's all it came down to. He changed moods like he was going through the menopause."

While it was a slightly less wholesome interpretation, Katy's frustration with men who couldn't decide whether to declare their undying love or to back off altogether was a major theme of her teenage years.

"Y'know, guys don't get the picture that us women love them and that we love them eternally, and some younger guys don't get that we want consistency every once in a while," she told *Tideline*. "I was seeing a guy who was definitely like, 'Yeah, I'm gonna take you to dinner – and for me, those words meant, 'Shower. Shave. Everything. Nails. Dress. Feet.' And then, all of a sudden, 8pm comes round and he's like out with his dudes and you're like, 'Oh my God, I just went through this whole transformation and I HATE YOU! DO YOU KNOW HOW MUCH THIS MAKE-UP COSTS?!'"

As a woman, Katy longs to be appreciated and admired, yet in 'Self Inflicted', when she compares a torturous love affair to crowd-surfing at a rough and tumble rock show, she's definitely one of the boys again. Katy constantly walks a tightrope between two worlds. Tomboy or glamour puss? Sex kitten or young lady? Bible-worshipper or fallen woman? Does she want to kiss boys or girls – or not at all? What is worthy of God-like status in her life – sex, music, love or the man Himself? Whatever her answers, she changes as often as her boyfriend in 'Hot And Cold', who is prone to bipolar mood swings.

'Lost' reveals a softer side to Katy. While 'If You Can Afford Me' portrays someone as hard as nails, in 'Lost', she has a candy-coated centre. Penned during tough times between record deals, she talks of the temptation to return home to the safety and comfort of her family, yet by now she is so lost that she cannot find the way back – the way is gone.

'I'm Still Breathing' speaks of a similar confusion. Alone in LA, Katy loses the man she loves. Funereal references convey the ending of her relationship with Matt Thiessen, along with tales of a sickness that has no cure. In desperation, she questions whether she is to blame – was she too curvaceous, or too pale-skinned?

Co-writer David Allan Stewart had also produced Katy's earlier song 'All I'm Selling Is Sex', but on 'I'm Still Breathing', he had returned to the dark, tragedy-tinged songs for which he was renowned. He described the song as "the only really sad and melancholic [one] on the album".

'Fingerprints' is another of Katy's early songs, which voices her frustration at working for Taxi to earn barely more than the minimum wage. She hints at a sordid lifestyle on the road to fame, begging on the Los Angeles streets and "trading under-table favours" to scrape up enough cash for a place to sleep.

It was co-written with Scott Cutler, who had previously worked on Beyoncé's 'Listen' and was renowned for his dramatic power ballads. Under this theme, Katy tells of plucking up the courage to take control of her own life and become the star she'd always wanted to be. The storyline is similar to 'When I Grow Up' by The Pussycat Dolls and Lady Gaga's 'The Fame', but Katy's yearning for recognition takes on a more sinister tone.

Yet the album ends on a positive note with 'I Think I'm Ready' where she discusses opening her heart in readiness to receive true love – the one great love affair she'd dreamed of since childhood. Lyrically, in Katy's chaste earlier days, she had promised to give her life over to God and devote herself to His word, yet she was now telling suitors they could never win the key to her underpants unless they could afford her. She had transformed herself from a nun to a prostitute and back again, all through her songs. Katy was a bundle of contradictions – just the way she liked it – but what would the mass media make of her debut into pop?

First Katy faced accusations of plagiarism. The country artist Gretchen Wilson had released an album by the same name just a year earlier, featuring lyrics like, "I know I don't act much like a lady, but I still need to be someone's baby" – Katy's sentiments exactly. This raised the question of whether Katy was just another bland country music rebel, manufactured in the style of Avril Lavigne and intended to shock onlookers with her angel-whore transformation. Could it be that she was just another good Christian girl gone bad?

Glen Ballard thought otherwise. "Nobody got what she was about," he insisted. "She had talent, personality, humour, a sense of fashion. [People] didn't know what to do with it."

Katy had to fend off more criticism from *AllMusic*, which typecast her as a talentless attention seeker. "The 24-year-old trollop is singing with the desperation of a fading burlesque star twice her age," the website claimed. "[She is] some ungodly hybrid of Alanis Morissette's caterwauling and the cold calculation of Britney Spears in her prime." The review went on to suggest that, due to her connections with writers who had penned tracks for both artists, she was merely a manufactured product under her producers' control.

Yet alongside the corporate company directors rubbing their hands together at the thought of profit, the website claimed that Katy was perhaps the worst contender of all. "All of the pros give *One Of The Boys* a cross-platform appeal," the review continued, "but there's little question that its revolting personality is all down to Katy Perry, who distills every reprehensible thing about the age of *The Hills* into one album. She disses her boyfriend with gay-baiting, she makes out with a girl and she doesn't even like girls, she... parties till she's face down in the porcelain, drops brands as if they were weapons, curses casually and trades under the table favours – her vile wild-child persona is an artifice designed to get her the stardom she craves."

NME was even less complimentary, awarding the album three out of ten points. "Perry is no genuine provocateur, rather than another ambitious woman reared on a childhood of church performance," it claimed. "Like Beyoncé and Christina, she clearly fell more deeply in love with the spotlight than Christianity." It added: "This record is unremarkably dire. It's as mundanely malevolent as stepping in a turd or getting stung by a bee... if you've got even a passing interest in actually enjoying a record, don't buy this one."

In spite of these disappointments, she received praise from *Uncut* magazine, which boasted, "Gwen Stefani should be nervous" and from the enamoured *Blog Critics*, which claimed: "*One of the Boys* is 12 tracks of pure pop bliss... [it] puts the high-profile release of Madonna to shame. There isn't a single bad song on the disc."

Finally, while the likes of *NME* dismissed her as a manufactured pop tart, *Blog Critics* countered that by writing: "In an industry plagued with cookie-cutter corporate groups, Katy Perry stands out like a beacon in rough seas."

There would certainly be rough seas ahead for Katy, as – just three days after the release of the album – she embarked on the USA's biggest ever annual punk festival.

The Warped Tour was a 10-week circuit of America, tirelessly bringing punk music to the masses. Katy had once told *INK19*: "A lot of my friends are in bands and they're on the road 200 days a year and they're dying of heart attacks at age 25. We'd like to go where we're wanted, not where we're not wanted."

Potentially, however, this was the type of heart-attack tour that Katy had been talking about – and one thing was for sure, it was no place for a girl who took style tips from Lolita.

Many of the fans who attended had some aggression to release and craved a hardcore punk sound – but what they would get was Katy fluttering her eyelashes coquettishly, wearing pink and singing love songs. It wasn't an exclusively male environment – Hayley Williams, the flame-haired singer of Paramore, had been the star of the previous year's show. However she had offered a harder rock sound, something that Katy was seriously lacking. Her sarcastic jokes might have appealed but she was still selling candy-coated, sugar-saturated pop. What was more, her audience certainly wouldn't be acting gay in response.

Understandably, Katy was uncertain that The Warped Tour was the right match for her music. "I'm really scared because there's a lot of boys on that tour and not a whole lot of women," she told *AZ Central*. "I also thought to myself: I'm a pop girl on a major label and I get the opportunity to do something as cool as The Warped Tour, and not have to open up for some lame-ass singer."

It was a double-edged sword for Katy, then – it would introduce her to a wider audience, but she also risked being booed off the stage. Yet with 100 punk bands lined up across 10 different stages, perhaps there was something for everyone.

Despite her doubts and obsession with how she might smell, Katy got into the spirit of the event. She claimed: "I'm scared because I heard that you don't get to shower every day, so I'll be bringing baby powder everywhere. If you're coming to The Warped Tour, please bring me perfume bottles. It's going to be a lot of boys, a lot of smelly boys [but] it's going to be a lot of fun. I'm excited."

What was more, just eight years earlier, her idol Gwen Stefani had graced the same stage with No Doubt. "I'm hoping to try and step in her shoes a little bit on Warped and 10 years later, have a hot husband, a couple of babies and rule the world," Katy grinned. "Gwen Stefani did the tour back in 2000 and she looked fabulous hopping around on stage in her little polka-dotted dresses. I'm so channelling that."

Katy started shows by bounding onto the stage with a cartwheel, looking like a teenage vintage pin-up girl – and almost invariably attracting cries of delight from the audience. She had her war paint on, her polka-dot skirts as part of the tribute she'd promised to No Doubt, pastel-shaded tops and heart-motif belts. It was hard to imagine how Katy, who styled herself on the Stanley Kubrick film version of *Lolita*, would blend in enough to be accepted by thousands of demanding rock fans. However, her looks were deceptive. Underneath the kitsch, Katy combined child-like playfulness with a gritty, ruthless determination you wouldn't find in the average businessman, let alone a child. She wanted to prove her survival skills against the rockers, but do it while looking sensational at the same time.

She had some competition for her harajuku-themed look in the shape of Oreskaband – an all-female Japanese ska group. They could be good company for Katy as, potentially equally ill-fitted to the tour, they could share in their mutual kitschiness – a rarity at a punk show – and console each other if their pop antics were booed off the stage.

The band sang entirely in their native language and, like Katy, weren't afraid to play up their good looks. According to one blogger, the six teenage girls "churned out relentlessly happy-sounding songs that had even the mohawked, tattooed audience members nodding their heads to the beat".

Katy hoped to become that infectious too, explaining to *Chron* magazine, "I'm eager to prove to people that, even though I'm a pop artist on a major label, I'm legit. I play my guitar and the band rocks and I want to earn the respect of everyone out there." While Oreskaband might have been there to offer consolation if she failed, failure wasn't a word in the hot-headed young Katy's vocabulary.

She had a carefully planned strategy for anyone who disrespected her: "I wave and I say, 'Hi, haters!' I smile really large and then I laugh all the way to the bank!"

She continued to *Chron*: "I think that The Warped Tour is a challenge and a test for me. I am loading some of my own equipment. I'm walking the half mile to the venue, just like everybody else. There's no golf-cart service. The humidity is hard to breathe in sometimes. There's dust. We get no soundcheck. If I can do this, I feel like I can probably do any tour."

Somehow Katy had made a simple punk festival sound as arduous as crossing the Kalahari desert without water. Perhaps she was practising to become a diva ahead of her time. Moving on to bigger things was certainly the plan, as she continued: "I'll have that tour, hopefully in the future, where we can have really high production values and I'll actually be able to hear what I'm singing!"

She might have had visions of a luxurious tour packed with glamour, but for now she was happy to let her fantasies take a back seat. In spite of her plentiful supply of perfume, pretty clothes and baby wipes, she was going to become one of the boys. "I have bruises all over my legs," a thrilled Katy boasted to *Rolling Stone*. "That's from wearing leggings. I'm jumping off the monitors and doing scissor-kicks or trying to keep up with these boys. It's funny. There's another stage going on right before I go on and usually it's like a hardcore screamo band with a mosh pit spanning the size of an arena and I've got all pink gear and a soft pink bubblegum guitar. I definitely am keeping up with them, but I am causing injury at the same time."

Katy survived the testosterone-fuelled tour by taking two female companions with her. The pair not only entertained her with a sense of humour sarcastic enough to match her own but also, according to Katy, made her ovulation stay intact.

As well as female company, Katy also had a new love interest, Travis McCoy, who was also playing on The Warped Tour with his band Gym Class Heroes. She had first met him in a tiny, windowless New York recording studio, where the two shared the same producer. Sparks didn't fly initially, however. "We didn't pay each other much attention because we were very focused on getting the songs done, but at the end of my trip – it was just when I first started going to New York and not really knowing anybody – I was like, 'Please, God, somebody take me out.' So I made him take me out," she told *Alloy*.

Her alpha-female role appealed to Travis, who was already hooked. "I was smitten as soon as she walked in the room," he recalled. "She's a girl who demands attention. I have no game whatsoever, so I decided, 'I'm just gonna ignore the shit out of her.'"

This only made the attention addict more keen. An alcohol-fuelled night followed where the two ended up "dancing and making out on the dance floor". They then embarked on a long-distance relationship with both travelling regularly between New York and Los Angeles – and Katy felt The Warped Tour was the ideal opportunity to strengthen their bond and start to date formally. "Let's be boyfriend and girlfriend," she told him. Was the gesture a romantic one or was it simply a relationship of convenience? Only time would tell.

However, she found him useful when fending off her punk rock admirers. "My boyfriend is 6' 5" and covered in tattoos so I don't get a whole lot of attention from guys," she told *Digital Spy*. "They're pretty much scared shitless!"

Meanwhile Katy found herself in the embarrassing situation of sharing the bill with her ex-boyfriend. Matt Thiessen was also on tour with his group, Relient K. His slot was no surprise – *The New York Times* had claimed: "Except for their devotional lyrics, the band sounds indistinguishable from a secular rock group."

However, Katy would now be performing 'Thinking Of You' and 'I'm Still Breathing' – odes to her relationship with Matt – in front of him, before returning to her new beau as soon as she left the stage.

Rumours circulated that not only had Katy dated Matt, but she had also had a fling with the guitarist in his band, Matt Hoopes. Perhaps the tales of her bed-hopping were little more than idle rumours, but it made for some uncomfortable moments.

Katy occupied herself during awkward times by checking out other bands on the tour. She even jumped onstage with long-haired rock singer Andrew WK, an experience she would go on to describe as "the best thing of my life". She told *Rolling Stone*: "There was only room for maybe 25 people on stage, but there were 125 people on stage. People were lifting their shirts, showing their belly, stagediving. It was like Sodom and Gomorrah."

With all Katy's Biblical references, it was clear that even if the girl was taken out of the Bible belt, the Bible belt couldn't be taken out of the girl – even in the sweaty punk-rock atmosphere of Warped Tour land.

On the Canadian leg of the tour, she had an even more fun experience. "I was grabbing some food with my band at this restaurant. We were just eating and I noticed the waiters had this quote on the back of their shirts and this quote said 'I've kissed more girls than Katy Perry.' It was the most random thing I've ever seen in my life! I was like, 'What's happening? Who did this? Is this a joke? Am I being Punk'd right now?' When I see little things like that, I think 'What did I do?'" she laughed to *Digital Spy*.

Katy was already well on the way to becoming a household name. She wooed America city by city, until the tour ended on August 17. One of the final reviews she received was from an enthused blogger. "Katy Perry is an anomaly on this tour for several reasons: she is a woman, she is a pop singer and she has a song which has spent the last month atop the *Billboard* singles chart," he began incredulously. Yet he conceded: "In spite of a teal top, matching shorts and perfect hair, she played to the scene, rolling around the stage like a rock star and leading her band in heavier, more guitar-driven arrangements of her songs. By the time she closed with her big hit, boys were singing along and dozens of girls were crowd-surfing. On this day it was not the least punk thing to happen."

Praise indeed for Katy – and definitely the validation she'd hoped for. Even with a pink parasol and a giant pink unicorn as regular onstage props, The Warped Tour was accepting her as she was. However it was the incident in the restaurant that she had enjoyed the most – the ideal way to end the tour.

After the long weeks of back-to-basics camping, Katy was more than ready to have her appetite for glamour satisfied – and there was no better place for that than the 2008 Video Music Awards on September 7. Despite her virtual obscurity just a few months earlier, she found herself nominated for five awards – Best New Artist, Best Art Direction, Best Cinematography, Best Editing and Best Female Video for 'I Kissed A Girl'. The nominations gave a middle finger to critics who believed her track had been successful purely for shock value. Katy wanted to prove she wasn't a gimmick but an entertainer – and, beyond that, she was also a meaningful artist in her own right.

Although she wasn't successful on the night, the VMAs were special for another reason – Katy would have her first meeting with the man who would become her husband, the host for the show, Russell Brand, the British comedian who was at that point almost unheard of in the USA. He was launching his career in America just as Katy was, and would be showing off a series of his trademark jokes throughout the show.

Katy was on the receiving end of one such joke when he introduced 'I Kissed A Girl' with, "Oh my God! I was so inspired by Katy Perry's song message that I'm currently going through nine chapsticks a day and my penis has never felt more moisturised!" he quipped.

He claimed to *The Sun* later than he'd had to curb the urge to shout out a potentially career-destroying comment during the ceremony, but it seemed as though he might already have done that, as his comments became increasingly outrageous throughout the evening.

The Jonas Brothers were devout evangelical Christians from a similar background to Katy's, with a pastor father and a stay-at-home mother who had home-schooled them to eliminate unwholesome influences. All wore purity rings, promising to abstain from sex until marriage. They also shunned alcohol. Russell could not claim the same – and a bit of red wine only got his creative juices flowing. As they took to the stage, he found the perfect way to ridicule them.

Holding up a ring, he exclaimed: "Well done, Jonas Brothers! God bless those boys! In case you're wondering, each of the Jonas Brothers wears [a purity ring] to show their commitment to God! I would take them more seriously if they wore it around their genitals!"

He added: "It is a little ungrateful to be able to have sex with any teenager in the world, but they won't! They're not gonna do it! It's like Superman deciding not to fly to save people in a bus. Listen, lads, it really is a weird way to control a boy band!" In his second reference to Katy of the evening, he then cackled: "There's gonna be Katy Perry singing 'Like A Virgin' and Jonas Brothers just pretending!"

His comments followed a *South Park* episode which portrayed the brothers as hypocrites, selling the message of purity to make themselves seem even more sexually alluring. A spoof concert featured teenagers screaming hysterically and rubbing themselves against chairs, all the while singing along to their lyrics about waiting until marriage. The brothers then appeared on a breakfast TV show, to be told by an admiring host: "It's good that little girls can see a concert and not have it be about sex. We understand that, at the concert tonight, you'll be dousing girls in the audience with white foam."

One young boy on the cartoon, on hearing about a ring that allows couples to be together but not to have sex, asked: "Isn't that called a wedding ring?" Perhaps Russell had taken inspiration from the *South Park* episode.

At one of his comedy shows in New York, Russell had raised the subject by saying: "The Jonas Brothers' chastity rings and virginity might in fact be a cynical marketing ploy utilising the themes of [philosopher] Michael Foucault who said that in Victorian society, the repression of sexuality was just another way of bringing sexuality to the forefront of our consciousness. It's a marketing technique. By saying that The Jonas Brothers are virgins, you can't help but think about them having sex!"

While his comments received a warm welcome at the comedy night, the response at the family-friendly VMAs was open hostility. *American Idol* winner Jordin Sparks arrived on stage 10 minutes later to challenge:

"It's not bad to wear a promise ring, because not everybody – guy or girl – wants to be a slut." Even Paris Hilton of porn video fame defended the brothers, saying: "I don't pick on them. That's something cool for a kid to keep, so don't pick on them for that."

Moments later, Russell himself apologised profusely, but got himself into more hot water in the process. "I've gotta say sorry," he told his audience. "That was bad of me. I didn't mean to take it lightly. I love Jonas Brothers, I think it's really good. I don't want to piss off teenage fans – I want to do the opposite of that. By the opposite of that, I don't mean I want to piss on teenage fans..." Russell was, quite deliberately, digging himself a deeper hole.

He added: "Promise rings, I'm well up for it, well done everyone... it's just a bit of sex occasionally never hurt anyone."

A disgruntled American blogger hit out at him, arguing: "He is a low-life scumbag who has had his brain damaged by hard living. He makes Amy Winehouse look classy. We do not want that slime bucket here in the USA."

Some responses were of outrage and indignation, while other viewers found his jokes hysterically funny. Perhaps surprisingly, Katy was one of the latter. Soon afterwards, she told *BBC Radio 1* that she'd fallen in love with him. "I met Russell Brand who I'm in love with," she revealed. "I love him, he's so great. He's got the worst sense of humour in the best sense of the way."

In fact, Katy had been making her own jokes about chastity. She had told the press: "I've actually taken a vow of celibacy this year – no kissing anyone, just my cat Kitty Purry."

Taking her religious background into account, several newspapers believed she was serious. She set the record straight later for *Beliefnet,* clarifying: "By the way, that was a joke and any fine journalist would have got that joke. I'm not going to be celibate. I guess I'm just going to be looking for the right one, but please – celibacy for a whole year? I would rather die."

Besides his jokes, which he believed were an aphrodisiac to women, Russell had also made a personal approach to Katy on the evening of the VMAs, so he was doubtless pleased to learn that she was definitely not celibate. He had been rounding up potential targets for a cameo in his forthcoming film, *Get Him To The Greek*. The role would involve kissing Russell, so he was on the lookout for sexy female celebrities. His criteria? It wasn't acting ability or stage presence that he sought – he only asked that they be gorgeous, and Katy fitted the bill.

He showered Katy with compliments, which she had taken with a pinch of salt – after all, at the same ceremony, he'd pledged to impregnate Britney Spears and declared that Christina Aguilera was "the perfect object". Were his comments misogynistic or just flirtatious banter? Either way, Katy was paying little attention, knowing that a double dose of his humour would be directed at everyone that night.

Yet she understood his dry wit, in contrast to many other Americans. Russell was the English answer to Eminem, who had rapped about impregnating The Spice Girls, boasted that he would have had sex with Jennifer Lopez even if she had been his own mother, and accused Christina Aguilera of giving other musicians sexually transmitted diseases. Russell was controversial – and while some Americans found his jokes about as appealing as scaling an electric fence, Katy found herself charmed by it.

What was more, although Katy was taken, there was trouble in paradise already. The cracks began to show in her relationship with Travis when she angrily reprimanded a group of girls in the VMA backstage area, who had dared to flirt with her beau. According to eyewitnesses, she had screamed, "Why don't you whores just piss off?"

Perhaps a little under her thumb, Travis had then nervously averted his eyes from all women for the rest of the evening. Russell was desperate to fill Travis's shoes, but he had to be content with befriending Katy.

There can be no question that on the surface they were chalk and cheese. Russell's chequered past had seen him described as a serial womaniser, a former heroin and crack cocaine user, a sex addict devoid of morals who tackles the unspeakable topics of sex, politics and religion in public. Katy's parents would have been horrified: he was about as far removed from their religious ideal as could be imagined, but Katy accepted the invitation to take part in his film regardless.

In the event, he temporarily faded from her radar as she set off for the next stage of her tour in one of her favourite cities, London. In fact, it would be almost a year before the two would cross paths again and in the meantime Katy was firmly focused on her next show – at a dingy Hackney pub known as The Water Rats, on September 10, in front of just 200 people.

The pub where she made her UK debut was overcrowded and full of the stench of alcohol and sweat. The surrounding area was the heart of gritty East London – not the first stop of anyone's tourist itinerary. In spite of this, she held her head up high, hoping it was just the beginning and a passport to better things.

Her positive attitude worked, and Katy already had the girls seduced. One admirer on the music website *Get Glucky* gushed: "Now I know this sounds like a completely macho pig thing to say – and I'm not male and hopefully not a pig – but my GOSH is Katy Perry hot. It's really hard not to notice."

Katy played up to her female admirers, teasing them by making a fake call to her mother during the concert. "Mom, I did kiss a girl but the only reason I did was... because she was fucking hot!" she screamed into her mobile.

Women entering the venue were also rewarded with a promotional cherry chapstick as a novelty item. Perhaps the occasional metrosexual man grabbed one too. This was about the only glamorous thing in the show but despite her longing for big production values and props, she needn't have been nervous. Even without the glitter and glitz, her voice was appealing to reviewers all on its own. *The Sunday Mirror* saw beauty in the simplicity of her set-up, praising: "Backed up by a four-piece band, but without any fancy lights or expensive backing singers, the stripped-back intimate nature of the show let her very fine pop voice shine."

There was further praise for Katy about her wit, which matched the British sentiment. "Katy clearly has a sense of humour and doesn't take herself too seriously, something all too often lacking in American poppettes," the review continued. "Katy was fizzing with energy, impish bonhomie and cheeky repartee with the crowd." The most glowing praise of all was the suggestion that Katy would transform from a starstruck young girl in a London pub to a fully-fledged performer at Wembley one day.

The Evening Standard was equally impressed, saying: "Her vibrant performance showed real star quality and could win over a crowd 10 times bigger than this one. There was no need for a talent this big to start her London assault this small."

Katy reciprocated London's love, screaming: "Thanks for popping my cork, it's been really messy! I love this city and I want to get a flat here." The stream of forlorn fans waiting outside the pub, desperate to get a ticket, showed how quickly her fame had risen. Her mammoth-size tour bus almost dwarfed the pub it stood beside. Promoters were left bewildered at how they might fit a personality of her size into the venue.

A far cry from the volleys of criticism she'd received in recent months, the only question now on everyone's lips was why an artist who'd held the number one spot in Britain's charts for the past five weeks was playing her first London show in a tiny back room of a pub and charging just £7.50.

KATY SHOWS OFF TWO GONGS AT THE 2009 EUROPE MUSIC AWARDS AT BERLIN'S 02 ARENA ON NOVEMBER 4. (DAVE HOGAN/GETTY IMAGES)

KATY ROCKS THE 2010 MTV MOVIE AWARDS AT UNIVERSAL STUDIOS' GIBSON AMPHITHEATRE, CALIFORNIA ON JUNE 6, WEARING AN ELECTRIC BLUE SMURFS WIG AND MATCHING BLUE HOT PANTS. (CHRISTOPHER POLK/GETTY IMAGES)

IT'S ANOTHER GAGA THEMED OUTFIT AS KATY DONS A CARNIVAL-STYLE HEAD-DRESS
FOR NEW YORK'S 2010 VICTORIA'S SECRET FASHION SHOW. (THEO WARGO/GETTY IMAGES)

INSET: KATY HONOURS THE "MAN UPSTAIRS" WITH THE "JESUS" SLOGAN SHE HAD TATTOOED ACROSS HER WRIST AT AGE 17.

ARMED WITH A BRIGHTLY COLOURED LOLLIPOP, KATY DELIVERS A SUGARY DIET THAT WON'T ROT YOUR TEETH. ON STAGE AT NBC'S TODAY SHOW ON AUGUST 27, 2010. (KEVIN MAZUR/GETTY IMAGES)

KATY SHINES IN A SHIMMERY RED CATSUIT AT LA'S 2010 AMERICAN MUSIC AWARDS ON NOVEMBER 21. (LESTER COHEN/GETTY IMAGES)

KATY ROCKS THE MARINE THEME AT THE LIFE BALL, HELD AT VIENNA'S RATHAUS ON MAY 17, 2008, TO RAISE MONEY FOR HIV AND AIDS VICTIMS. (FLORIAN SEEFRIED/GETTY IMAGES)

SEASHELLS AND STARFISH ADORN KATY'S CUSTOM MADE LEOTARD AS SHE PERFORMS AT VIENNA'S LIFE BALL. (FLORIAN SEEFRIED/GETTY IMAGES)

KATY'S BREASTS HAVE EYES AS SHE ARRIVES IN LIVERPOOL FOR THE 2008 MTV EUROPE MUSIC AWARDS IN LIVERPOOL ON NOVEMBER 6 IN YET ANOTHER UNUSUAL CREATION. (LEON NEAL/AFP/GETTY IMAGES)

Chapter 7

The Edge Of The Knife

Katy's success continued with the release of second single 'Hot And Cold'. It was an instant hit.

Her soft rock voice captured the angst of The Pretty Reckless, the moody indie tones of No Doubt and the very essence of Courtney Love on tranquillisers. The video was equally lively, giving an angry Katy the opportunity to chase a lover with a team of bridesmaids wielding baseball bats. The object of her fury? A commitment-phobic husband to be who jilts her at the altar seconds before they become man and wife. Yet all's well that ends well when her fiancé awakens from his dream of rebellion and instead leads her dutifully down the aisle.

The single stormed the charts, earning the number two spot in Germany based on Internet downloads alone. It peaked at number one where it remained for eight consecutive weeks. She also made the top spot in Canada and peaked at number three in the USA and number four in the UK.

While her single was climbing the charts, she was embarking on her first ever Australian tour. In Sydney on October 10, Katy jumped atop one of the speakers before pulling her skirt up and revealing her pants, squealing: "There! Now you've got your picture!" When *AllMusic* said she would stop at nothing to get attention, it hadn't been exaggerating.

Perhaps her aim was to perk up the bored male members of her audience. Believing that they had been dragged there against their will by their persuasive other halves, she joked: "You must hate me! But you might get laid if you said, 'Yes baby, I'll come to the Katy Perry concert with you!', so you should be moving your hips!" It was a perfect introduction to the song 'If You Can Afford Me', although in this case, she was implying that her fans would sell themselves for the price of a Katy Perry ticket – the hottest show in town.

Less than a week later, on October 16, Katy was the centre of attention again – but this time on the opposite side of the globe, as she performed at the Latin America MTV Awards in Mexico. Never one to shy from the spotlight, she was dressed in a huge billowing dress of the type seen in *My Big Fat Gypsy Wedding*. Plus, despite her hardcore globe-trotting, she still had enough energy left for mischief.

At the end of her performance of 'I Kissed A Girl', Katy was planning to leap head-first into a giant cake but disaster struck when she slipped on the pastel-pink icing sugar, almost losing one of her flimsy ballet pumps in the process. Red-faced and covered in confectionery, she went flying across the stage – a memorable exit indeed. Whether she intended it or not, Katy could always pull the crowds. In fact, onlookers compared the scene to a brunette Alice in Wonderland tumbling down the rabbit hole.

On her return to the UK Katy had a nasty surprise – her face was plastered all over the British tabloids, amid a wave of disapproval. In the offending photograph, she was holding a flick knife. The 2005 photo shoot, which Katy had thought was long forgotten, had taken place more than three years earlier as promotion for her ill-fated album with Columbia. The CD had never hit the shelves and the pictures had been discarded – or so she thought.

Terry Richardson, the man responsible for the shoot, was a photographer with a reputation for pushing the boundaries. A veteran at portraying raw sexuality in all its forms, he had even persuaded top fashion models to pose nude for his camera. He wasn't afraid to explore elements of violence either. It was in a shoot by Terry that Amy Winehouse had casually carved her husband's name into her stomach with shards of glass. The image, originally intended for *Spin* magazine, had hit headlines worldwide.

Terry was unshockable. He had persuasive charm, an unconventional creative instinct and a keen sense of mischief. Combined with Katy, the pair's mischief had known no bounds – and now her face was emblazoned across *The Sun* newspaper, holding a knife perilously close to her throat. A source told *The Sun*: "The knife picture was done to give Katy more of a sexy, harder edge. But in the end, it wasn't picked as a main shot for her album or website."

The timing could not have been worse: Britain was experiencing a brutal wave of knife crime that year, with more than 60 deaths from stabbings. Tragically, many of the fatalities were teenagers.

Just as 'Ur So Gay' had been released at the same time as a young boy had been beaten to death over his sexuality in Liverpool, the knife picture would hit raw nerves in "Broken Britain" too. At the time that the picture hit the news-stands, two of Katy's songs were in the UK charts – 'I Kissed A Girl' was at number 14, with 'Hot And Cold' close behind. There was concern that a high-profile celebrity posing with a blade would glamorise the culture of carrying knives. Anti-knife campaigner Richard Taylor, whose son Damilola had been murdered on a South London housing estate eight years previously, raged: "There is nothing glamorous about knives – they wreck families. Any youngster seeing her will think it is OK to carry a blade."

Actress Brooke Kinsella, whose younger brother was a more recent knife victim, echoed: "Celebrities are role models, so their management and record label should think about the consequences."

Yet, for Katy, it was a mystery how the pictures had surfaced. Taken when she was signed to a different record label, it seemed that someone released the pictures to boost Katy's notoriety. Had their release been deliberately timed to coincide with the trend in knife attacks to make them seem all the more controversial? Could it even have been sour grapes from someone who'd got hold of the pictures and resented her success? If so, who was responsible?

Katy was publicly remorseful, telling *Now* magazine: "I never tried to hide anything. I'm a pop girl, I play music and I want to make people happy." She added "When I saw the picture, it was a big deal – especially for you guys. I feel really bad. It was just a misunderstanding."

However, with all the tenacity of Russell Brand trying to promote a lewd joke in a room full of nuns, Katy then got her own back, using her blog. She posed for a picture with a spoon pressed to her cheek alongside the slogan: "I don't condone knife use, but I do condone eating ice-cream with a very large spoon." She then wrote an open letter to *The Sun,* blasting: "You deserve a time out. Your 'journalistic' approach has half the soul of *The National Enquirer.* Shame on you."

Richard Taylor was despondent, begging for a more sincere apology. "Youngsters would have seen that and taken it as something positive," he said. "Instead she has decided to challenge us."

An anonymous source told the author: "Katy received some very unpleasant Internet messages after that fiasco. Yet Angelina Jolie gave a knife to her son when he was six and has admitted having knife fights with her lovers, even though she says she wants to be a responsible parent. For some reason, with all this craziness going on around her, it was Katy who took all the anger for what was going on in England."

Indeed, there were even calls for her to be dropped from the European Music Awards on November 6, which she had agreed to host that year, as it was deemed that she was a bad role model. However Katy didn't feel she needed to apologise. She told *Alloy*: "I would look into the music industry and see a void there for a movement of female artists that were unapologetic, that had something to say."

Another comment revealed exactly the kind of attitude that was guiding her behaviour. "I'm not here to be a role model personality," she told *YRB* magazine. "I'm here to be in the business of fucking rock 'n' roll. Being in the business of rock 'n' roll means having an attitude, being sexy, being edgy and being unapologetic, unless I do something wrong. I look up to people like Joan Jett, Pat Benatar, Freddie Mercury and Cyndi Lauper. If people want a role model, they can have Miley Cyrus."

An unlikely source of support was Matthew Turner, the Christian journalist who had interviewed her back in her Katy Hudson days. "We as humans are all in process," he told the author. "We live and grow and make mistakes and learn – the only difference with Katy is that she's doing it in the public eye."

Although she was unrepentant over the spoon joke, she still made it to the EMAs, riding on stage atop a giant cherry chapstick to the delight of 10,000 spectators in the *Liverpool Echo* Arena.

It might have been a European event, but it was dominated by American artists, with Pink, Britney, Beyoncé and of course Katy all stealing the show. She proved that by coming out in a bright yellow dress emblazoned with President Obama's face on the front – just one of 12 outfit changes she would make that evening. Another costume included a hot pink romper suit with feather boa sprinkles, customised with the letters of her name. It was accompanied by a multicoloured dress with a carousel making up the skirt, a banana costume, and an outfit that comprised one half dress and one half trouser suit. Katy was teasing onlookers with ambiguity – was she a girl or was she in fact one of the boys?

Yet her attempts at cross-dressing paled in comparison to the reception she received when claiming the gong for Best New Act. Just a year ago she had been a virtual newcomer at the end of her tether, clinging on to the chance of a record deal by the skin of her teeth. Now she was accepting awards and travelling as far afield as South America, Europe and Australia. However, Katy was also becoming increasingly loose-lipped as her fame grew, firing verbal missiles at a range of targets.

She had joked that she dreamed of kissing Miley Cyrus and would have been happy to relive the famous Britney-Madonna kiss in a bid to boost her career, but had later belittled her, telling the media she was just another example of cookie-cutter pop. The next target on the missile list was the British singing sensation Lily Allen.

The mud-slinging had begun a few months previously when Hollywood-based celebrity gossip blogger Perez Hilton had published quotes, allegedly from an industry insider, about her. "Lily Allen is peeved at Capitol," the quote read. "She feels like they've shoved her aside to focus all their energies on the new girl of the moment, Katy Perry." The quote also indicated that the office's main lobby had once had a framed photograph of Lily on display, which had since been replaced by a snap of Katy. Perez added "She's known these days more for being a tragic train-wreck than a musician. She knows it and that must hurt – ha ha ha ha!"

Lily responded that Capitol was her distributor, not her label, and that she had never heard of Katy Perry until reading his blog. "Not everyone's lives are fuelled by egos and jealousy," she wrote. "I read these posts on his website about anti-bullying campaigns and all these good causes and, while I used to enjoy reading his site, it seems to me that recently he has become what he hates so much – a bully. He bullies young, successful females. People usually bully people they're jealous of, so I'll let you come to your own conclusions on that one."

Were Hilton's comments fuelled by jealousy? Chris Anokute had told *Hit Quarters* once before that Katy dominated the company's attention, claiming: "I tried to sign more talent, but the truth is, the company was so focused on Katy Perry that it was hard for me to focus on anything else."

However, a crucial flaw in Hilton's argument was his track record. The previous year he had falsely reported the death of the Cuban president, Fidel Castro. When it emerged Castro was alive and well, he described the story as the biggest mistake of his career. The following year, he would claim that reports of Michael Jackson's death were a "publicity stunt", before sarcastically egging on ticket holders for his 50-date O2 Arena tour to get their money back. The post was sheepishly removed soon afterwards, to be replaced with an apology, but not before an estimated nine million people had read his words. It was fair to say that Hilton did not have a good track record for accuracy.

A few more messages were exchanged between him and Lily, with Hilton publishing a photograph of her and Katy together and deeming her "a liar" for not acknowledging that they knew each other. Lily defended herself by pointing out that her celebrity status meant she was constantly fending off requests to pose for pictures, and she still could not recall who Katy was.

That seemed to be the end of the dispute, until Katy was updating the "sounds like" section of her Myspace profile one day. In an ill-advised, hackle-raising moment, she described herself as a "fatter version of Amy Winehouse and a skinnier version of Lily Allen".

This time, Lily challenged her live on UK radio, countering: "I happen to know for a fact that Katy was signed as an American version of me. She was signed by my label in America as, 'We need to find something controversial and kooky like Lily Allen.' It's like, you're not English and you don't write your songs – shut up!"

Katy was questioned about it by *US* magazine, but dismissed her words as an affectionate joke. "Comedians are not necessarily to be taken super seriously," she said. In an interview with *The Herald Sun Australia*, she elaborated: "We are both quite different. She's got the cool, reggae, laid-back sensibility with kooky lyrics and a great sense of humour. My stuff is a little more rock and pop and somewhat more mainstream. I think we both have different things to offer. Is there bad blood? Not from me. I will continue to buy her records. She's actually looking great these days, pretty fit."

Katy had charmed her way out of a potentially explosive situation in the nick of time. Lily wrote on her Facebook page: "I have Katy Perry's phone number, someone did me a favour – I'm just waiting for her to open her mouth one more time and then it hits Facebook."

Katy was safe – but not for much longer. In December 2008, she was portrayed in a rape scene by the bisexual singer Amanda Palmer, frontwoman of The Dresden Dolls. Together with comedian Margaret Cho, she ravaged Katy as part of her stage show. A virtual version of her was dragged onstage, groped, kissed and violated with a dildo. Katy was then forced into a lesbian marriage, bound and gagged with her hands together, as a banner was raised behind them to reveal the words "Fuck Proposition Eight!", a reference to the statute that decreed that only marriage between a man and a woman is valid or recognised in California.

The Daily Profaner urged: "This reaches a new level of hilarity when one considers both Katy Perry's parents are pastors. Needless to say, you should go buy Amanda Palmer's new album so that she has the cash to continue annoying Christian conservatives everywhere."

The rape was a political protest for Amanda. Proposition Eight was passed in California state elections in November 2008, overturning previous rulings by forbidding same-sex marriage. Although Amanda was bisexual, not lesbian, it remained close to her heart – and she was angry that Katy seemed to be faking homo-eroticism.

Amanda wrote on her blog: "We wonder if she's cashing in on the recent cultural bi-manic 'girls gone wild' obsession. Some of the gays love it. Some of the gays hate it. I just wanted to make out with her. OK, and maybe tie her up with gaffer tape."

She was aggravated by the jokey phone calls to Katy's mother that would become a part of her nightly stage show, too. Katy would speak, as if into an imaginary phone, saying: "Hello? Mom? Yeah, I'm having fun. You heard what? That I was a lesbian? It was just one innocent kiss – you've had one of those!" She would also boast on stage about "touching a girl's boobies". To Amanda, kissing girls had become a gimmick, a novelty, a marketing tool.

Katy would play up to the speculation, beginning an interview with *Sunday Times Style* by asserting: "Before you ask, the answer is yes. I fucking kissed a girl!" In the same interview, she went on to insist she was aroused by the female form, before carefully adding that she would never actually get involved with a woman. "I look at [girls] and think, 'Oooh, I'm so turned on. What's happening?'... I'm attracted to cool, alternative women. But I'd only ever have a drink with them. I'm such a tease!"

Amanda objected to the all-talk portrayal of her sexuality, writing on Twitter: "My duet with Katy Perry will be called 'I kissed a girl and I liked it, but then I had to deal with her vagina and I didn't know what to do.'"

The interviewer from *Sunday Times Style* came to the same conclusion about her when she scrunched her nose up at the idea of trying girl-on-girl relationships for real. She wrote: "For all the talk, I'd wager if a real lesbian cornered her in a dark alley, she'd peg it as fast as her five-inch heels could carry her."

In perhaps the most direct indication so far that her use of lipstick lesbianism was benefiting her career, Katy joked to *Times Square Gossip*: "If I could kiss anyone, it would be Miley Cyrus. She's the lucky girl. It's cool to hear through the grapevine that she has my song as her ring-tone, although I think she's cheating on me. I think she might really go for it. We'll see. She's hosting The Teen Choice Awards and I'll be on the show... maybe we'll have another Britney-Madonna moment onstage. How hilarious would that be? Although I don't think it would help her career. However, it would definitely help mine!"

Katy certainly knew how to make friends, teasingly kissing her interviewer at lesbian magazine *Diva* and also locking lips with female fans in her audience. She knew how to endear herself to her admirers, leaving the *Diva* staff member exclaiming that she had wanted to hate her for her "homophobic songs" but, when she'd met her in person, had been seduced under her spell, finding her irresistibly charming.

However, was it all a big fake? Were people buying into an empty illusion? That was the question Amanda Palmer had been posing. Katy told the media that almost every teenage girl had kissed their best friends once or twice out of innocent exploration. If so, wouldn't this make it a widely relatable and highly marketable concept to sell to the mainstream? Or was it so commonplace that the whole idea would seem dull? Perhaps it was just Katy's music that was appealing to the masses, not the message.

Regardless of what women thought, she would always be able to rely on an enamoured male audience. Her song was not the first to broach the tricky subject of kissing girls, but it was the first to universally make it on to radio and pass the censors. A male crowd, desperate to fuel their fantasies of sapphic playmates, was almost guaranteed.

However, this theory might have been harsh. Was Katy forbidden from expressing a simple curiosity about the same sex? Did she have to commit to being either entirely straight or entirely gay to be taken seriously? Amanda Palmer herself enjoyed the attention of both men and women, after all. Yet to some, returning to boys after achieving a number one hit from a song about kissing girls, was nothing short of a criminal offence.

In fact, Katy had been photographed at an after-party following her London Scala show that year, enjoying some close contact with a girl. The two embraced and kissed each other on the lips – and Katy's friend was an Agyness Deyn lookalike, exactly her type. She told *The Times* admiringly: "She's a little punk rock Lolita. Beautiful face, beautiful shoulders" and now she was locking lips with her mirror image, a short-haired tomboy with pixie looks. Perhaps there was some reality in her sapphic stereotype after all.

Another clue was in Katy's younger life. Her main inspiration for 'I Kissed A Girl' had been a crush, as she told *The Herald Sun Australia*. "[I was] just inspired by the ultimate beauty and power of a woman and that can transcend all sexual boundaries for anyone," she said. "When there's just like an amazing creature that walks into a room, everyone just turns their heads and just appreciates this kind of spiritual beauty."

Yet that hadn't been Katy's only point of reference. While she had joked to the German magazine *Bravo*, "I kissed a girl and it was like kissing my arm! I didn't feel anything!", a friend of Katy's remembered a moment the two had enjoyed very differently.

"Katy and I were friends – not best, but we enjoyed each other's company," she told the author. "She was often at a loose end because she was living on her own in LA and between record deals. She'd get so down that she often didn't feel like working at all. At times, she would drink, sometimes quite heavily, and I would never hesitate to join her."

She continued, "I was surprised when our kiss happened, because Katy would often talk about boys – she was obsessed with them. It was a slow-burning friendship, so nothing happened straight away, but when it did... Katy was slow and sensual and I don't think she was getting her needs met in that way from male lovers she'd met since she moved out here. She liked kissing me because it reminded her of kissing herself, someone in tune with her enough to know just what she wanted. She insisted afterwards that she was straight, as if she felt guilty. I didn't! I don't think she is totally bisexual, but she certainly enjoyed it. There's no barrier when it comes to sexuality – it's totally fluid."

Perhaps Katy's tales of kissing girls weren't just to promote her album, then. However, with all the talk of same-sex romance, it wasn't long before her relationship with her beau, Travis, crumbled. Ultimately, Katy had wanted more than he could give. She felt he had offered her "soulless hook-ups" and that she wanted to be more than a series of one-night stands. In an effort to prove his loyalty to her, Travis had bought her a promise ring, had tattooed her initials on his ring finger – and, of course, the two had talked of marriage. He'd even pulled all the stops out on a romantic trip to Mexico as a Christmas gift – but Katy still wasn't impressed.

It didn't help matters that she was constantly busy touring and involved in publicity, which took her to a new city almost daily. On the other hand, Travis was not doing as well as he'd hoped in the music world, with his last single, 'Cookie Jar', falling to a measly number 55 in the *Billboard* charts. Katy, on the other hand, was topping the very same charts. A couple of months later, it would be announced that 'Hot And Cold' had gone three times platinum, with three million downloads sold in the USA alone.

The pressure of the various issues in their relationship proved too much to bear and they had parted by the New Year. Travis posted a caustic message on his blog soon afterwards, featuring rap lyrics from Main Source's 'Looking At The Front Door'. He raged: "We fight every night, now that's not kosher, I remember with bliss of when we were closer, and wake up to be greeted by an argument again, you act like you are 10."

Katy had barely found time to mourn her loss before she was back on the road again, and her next single, 'Thinking Of You', was well timed. Although it was originally intended for Matt Thiessen, it now fitted perfectly with how she felt about Travis.

A video had originally been shot two years previously by a friend, but their amateur film was no longer enough now that she was aiming for a commercial release. Instead, a new promo was produced. In it, Katy mourns a lover who was killed in France during the Second World War, and struggles to focus on her new romance as thoughts of her former relationship creep back into her mind. "I wrote the song after being in love for the first time," Katy told *Cleveland.com*. "None of that puppy love crap, but that, 'OK, we're young adults, should we get married?' love. In the back of my mind, I had this slow-down yellow stop light that said, 'I don't know if this is it. There's still a lot more things I want to try and accomplish in life.'"

Katy had tortured herself with her conflicting thoughts – both the desire to spread her wings and the wish to settle down in the security of a familiar and cherished relationship. However, how could she hope to spread her wings if she settled down with a good Christian boy from her childhood, without taking the time out to sample some of the world's more forbidden fruit? It wouldn't be easy to walk away, but it would be equally difficult to stay.

"I was really in love with this guy at the time," she continued, "so it was really hard for me to move on. As I was moving on and meeting other people, he was constantly there in the back of my mind. I was comparing these new dudes to this old guy, my past relationship, and it wouldn't go away."

The video matched that emotion, channelling a funereal atmosphere. The glamour and humour of Katy's previous videos were absent, as she wore a black face veil and prepared to give her ex-lover a send-off in the style of Amy Winehouse's video for 'Back To Black'.

The video, which was released on January 12, 2009, received more than 18 million hits on Youtube, and the song was even covered by The Jonas Brothers. Despite that, it was the worst performing song Katy had ever released in America, charting at its peak at just number 29.

Just a couple of weeks later, there was another disappointment. The Matrix team were keen to release the album she had recorded with them due to the success of *One Of The Boys*. Katy's response was lukewarm – she wanted to wait until the final single from her album was released to prevent her sales from being negatively affected, but The Matrix were reluctant to wait. They released it via their own website on January 21.

Katy triumphed at London's Brit Awards on February 18. The dramas of her knife pictures were long forgotten as Lionel Richie handed her the award for Best International Female Solo Artist. The show was watched by 5.49 million households, which was validation for Katy that Britain really did love her – or, at least, had the opportunity to see her in action now to decide for themselves. She dressed in a punk-rock style Hello Kitty corset for the ceremony. In spite of the cute cartoon cat on the front, it had the hint of a bondage theme, mirroring Katy's own contradictions. Was she a hard toffee or a soft-centred caramel? The code was becoming increasingly difficult to crack.

On the red carpet, Katy switched into a soft pink Marilyn Monroe-inspired gown, but her smile hid an uncomfortable secret – she had been sick most of the day. In fact, seconds after receiving her award, she had to rush off to vomit backstage, but not before delivering her acceptance speech. "I'm so sick right now, but they said I should show up because something special might happen," she explained to the audience. "I work pretty hard because I want to die right now." Moments later, she texted Perez Hilton, claiming that she had "puked", signing off with the words "Punk rock!"

As Katy's tour continued, a new rival appeared on the scene in the shape of Lady Gaga. Her answer to 'I Kissed A Girl' was 'Pokerface', a song featuring a woman who fantasised about making love to another girl while she was in her boyfriend's bed, and revelled in deceiving him, knowing that he was oblivious. Yet secret lesbian fantasies and catchy pop tracks were not the only assets she had to offer. Gaga quickly built up a large following that was enthralled by the combination of her Catholic Italian-American upbringing and the side of her that was a libertine, an ex-lap dancer, a heavy drug user and, ultimately, a work of art.

Her kooky sense of style matched Katy's – was there room for two costumed women in the hearts of pop music lovers? The two might have been competing in the style stakes, but Katy had begun to incorporate food into her clothing long before Gaga had debuted her famous meat dress, covering herself in slabs of steak from head to foot.

Katy started out more gently, with a dress that was adorned with fruit for the 2009 Grammy Awards. Her sense of style displayed itself again for the single 'Waking Up In Vegas'. She had decided it was single material on the advice of her idol John Mayer, who had told her it was his favourite tune on the album. Backstage at one of his concerts, it was rumoured that Katy had even taken her appreciation of the musician a step further, as gossip columns reported the two had been "touchy feely". Electricity aside, she decided to take him up on his advice.

The single was released on April 21, with an accompanying video. The glitter and glamour of a party night in Vegas soon fades as Katy wakes up in a dirty, cheap motel room with the mother of all hangovers. She falls prey to the fate of many visitors, losing most of her money after an overambitious game of poker. Katy and her lover are thrown out of their hotel room and resort to stealing food from a room-service tray. Eventually the pair find themselves back where they started – broke and unfulfilled in a distinctly unglamorous laundromat.

Yet in direct contrast to the financial destitution, the outfits were decadent. "I have to tell you one of my favourite things were these costumes," Katy told *Cleveland.com* about the video. "The famous Bob Mackie picked out three or four of these costumes. They're from his vintage collection. He came downstairs from his warehouse to meet my stylist and said, 'I really want to be a part of this.' He picked out the head dress, the gloves and the dress – the whole thing. It was some costumes from the eighties or seventies. Who knows? Cher might have worn it."

It was a return to form for Katy, reaching number 19 in the UK chart and peaking at number nine stateside. The song also notched up a record 20 million hits on Youtube. Clearly expressing herself through glitz and glamour was what Katy succeeded at best.

Her chart position was bolstered by an appearance on *American Idol*, where she performed the song dressed as Elvis. In an added twist, she shared her support for her favourite singer Adam Lambert on the show by embroidering his name into the cape she was wearing. "I couldn't believe she cared so much," an onlooker said. "Who would have thought Katy Perry even has time to listen to a lowly amateur, let alone make a public shout out for him through her clothes? Maybe she remembers how good it felt when her own song was acknowledged by Madonna, making all the effort worthwhile."

Katy's clothing was fast becoming her number one way to express herself. At The Life Ball in Vienna, an annual event designed to raise money for HIV and AIDS victims, she proved that more than ever. She blended in perfectly at the society event, which was also attended by ex-president Bill Clinton, until she was lowered from the rafters of the building in a giant seashell.

The Mail reported: "The singer seemed inspired by an intriguing mix of *The Little Mermaid* and [Botticelli painting] *The Birth of Venus*... then she shed her flowing fishtail gown to show off a sparkling one-piece costume that left very little to the imagination."

The barely there flesh-coloured leotard was adorned with starfish and other marine-themed creatures. The event, hosted on May 16, drew praise that saw her described as more beautiful than fellow guest Pamela Anderson. The organisers had hoped to raise over one million euros that would give poverty-stricken AIDS sufferers access to life-prolonging medicine and, as her mermaid outfit was broadcast across newspapers around the world, Katy played her own part in that.

The night before, she had dressed in a tight, cling-film style cat-suit at a party, leaving admirers open-mouthed – but she hadn't nearly finished yet. On May 30, she attended the Video Music Awards in Japan, where she donned her most outrageous outfit by far. While performing 'I Kissed A Girl', she brandished two paper fans before seductively shaking off her kimono to reveal a leotard embroidered with rows of sushi. Katy wanted to appreciate Japan's cultural heritage in a unique way – by incorporating it into a strip-tease. Her golden tan, black lipstick and poker-straight raven black hair with its long fringe could have seen Katy mistaken for a native herself. Her outfit raised peals of laughter from the audience, but it was in the same leotard that she picked up her award for Best Pop Video.

Despite her frenetic travelling and alpha-female tendency to put work first, Katy had also reunited with her ex-boyfriend Travis, but the reconciliation was to be brief. Travis had gushed to *The Mail*: "The break-up sucked. I keep thinking about if I had to go through it again and how terrible it would be. We were moving way too fast. I was being juvenile about the whole thing. Now it's easy breezy. I'm happy and really in love."

Regrettably, he spoke too soon and later that month, the pair would part for good. Katy then predicted her own fate, telling *Loaded* magazine: "I'm still available. I could have an English boyfriend." Intended as a flirtatious compliment, little did she know how true that would prove to be.

Chapter 8

The Owl And The Pussycat

Russell Brand got his wish – Katy kept her promise to appear in his new film, *Get Him To The Greek*. After all, she was no stranger to the acting world – her maternal uncle, Frank, had been a Hollywood-based producer and film director while her aunt Eleanor had worked as a scriptwriter. Consequently there was a double dose of drama in the family's DNA – and Katy jumped at the chance to join the ranks of her relatives.

It didn't hurt that the role required a screen kiss – Katy's school-girl-style crush from the previous year had not yet faded. The object of her affections was playing the lead role, channelling an out-of-control rock musician with a penchant for hard drugs and risky sex. A career breakdown, rape allegations, illegitimate children, drug smuggling, over-enthusiastic groupies and an Amy Winehouse-style meltdown were just a few of the problems that awaited him – on many counts, some might say Russell was not really acting.

However, it was the opportunity to kiss fellow stars of the music world that truly required little acting. He had been on the lookout for pop artists of the moment for the scene and Christina Aguilera had been a hot candidate, as he told *The Sun*. "Christina was amazing!" he marvelled. "She was unbelievable – a perfect object. How could you ever talk to her about anything other than sex?" He was disappointed when he had to narrow down the pop-star kissing scenes to just two, but chose Pink and Katy Perry.

"I got to snog them both in one day," he boasted. "Pink is a lovely woman – a forceful, sexy woman." Yet it was Katy who had really captured Russell's attention. "She is the kind of girl who would skip downstairs lightly," he recalled. "With both of them, I didn't act – the acting stopped."

The chemistry was mutual. "My scene called for me to make out with him and on the way down the stairs after the scene, I was hopping like a bunny!" she told *Glamour*. "I hop like a bunny when I'm happy. I get a bit child-like. He gives me the Christmas Eve jitters."

The fantasy was short-lived though, as Katy soon had to get back on the road, returning to London for a concert at the Shepherd's Bush Empire on July 31. However, perhaps some of Russell's humour had infected her, as she asked teenagers in the audience, "Who's here with their mom and dad tonight? I feel very influential at this crucial moment in your life", before urging them to shout "naughty" words in front of their parents.

Her demeanour was poles apart from the teenager who'd expressed anxiety at letting her fans down by being a bad role model, feeling that she was responsible for keeping them on the right path. It seemed Katy had finally swept her neuroses aside and become comfortable in her own skin.

Meanwhile, when a fan threw a stuffed Bagpuss toy on stage, she hurled it back, questioning with a wrinkle of her nose who would want "a cat that fat".

Her wit was not lost on *The Observer*, who gave her a rave review. "Perry's real magic comes from what so many singers lack – her personality," it said. "Perry, at 24, is still teenager rude – laconic, with a biting wit and a level of cheek usually only heard from the back row of a classroom... I may not have been down the front angling for a kiss, but I really, really liked her."

Katy also impressed at Chelmsford's V festival, where she entertained a 20,000-strong crowd by bounding onstage surrounded by pink flamingos. Her unusual props and pop princess demeanour stood out a mile among the indie and rock bands. Even *NME*, which had labelled Katy the worst-dressed woman two years in a row at its awards, had something positive to say. "[She wore] a pair of awesome spangly hot pants, the kind of which we doubt you'd ever see the chaps from Snow Patrol rocking [and] the whole spectacle is infinitely more entertaining than a bunch of banter-free boys shuffling around behind their guitars." The review also challenged the opinion that she was style over substance by hitting back: "If we ain't here to be entertained, what exactly are we here for?" Indeed, Katy could certainly entertain, and she worked hard in doing so.

After the V Festival, she made a flying visit to Australia, followed by a 26-hour flight back to Scotland to honour a concert at Glasgow's Barrowlands. Her gruelling schedule was beginning to get on top of her and, just as Amy Winehouse had done at the same airport two years earlier, she lashed out at the security team. It was a verbal assault rather than a physical one, however, provoked by a request to check five suitcases packed full of stage clothes for her trip. She later implied that the underpaid, overworked staff might have been a little jealous of her glamour and celebrity status and were desperate to make life difficult. "I swear, I never feel more like cattle than when I have to go through airport security," she wrote. "They hate their lives and they hate us for sure. By the last flight, the third time going through security, I lost it."

While she adored her job, the constant travelling did have its disadvantages. She was becoming increasingly pressured, but the one thing she was looking forward to was the forthcoming VMAs. "I'm excited because you can wear all kinds of crazy things," she enthused. "It's not like the other award shows where you have to be popular and pretty and stuff. I'd come and look like a real-life cat if I wanted to – or just a strawberry."

What was more, Katy would have another meeting with the man she'd been lusting after. An elaborate outfit might just be worth it. They'd kissed, but both barely knew each other – and that was something Russell was determined to change. However, on the day, Katy beat him to it. During rehearsals for the New York ceremony, she walked straight up to him and playfully lobbed a plastic bottle right at his head.

Russell was astonished. He was used to wearing the pants with women and, since his career had taken off, he had been surrounded by adoring groupies willing to give into his every whim. Here was a woman who challenged and belittled him, a strong, witty, playful woman who prided herself on being as much of a comedian as he was. For him, it was a career – for her it was an art-form, and the occasional insult was par for the course.

She'd even taunted that he was an easy target, due to his "ridiculous hair". Although his pride was wounded, Russell quickly hit back that her aim was impressive for someone blind enough to wear such a "ridiculous sweater". A string of insults followed, seeing Katy brand him a "lazy transvestite" and Russell claim that he was certainly feminine in comparison to her. However, both parties agreed that Katy had won the round fair and square.

To prove she was wearing the pants, Katy showed up onstage in some. Russell, who was hosting the event for the second year running, introduced her as she sang Queen's 'We Will Rock You'.

Some of his gags might not have impressed her that evening. He insulted her home country, comparing it to the UK and claiming, "Instead of 'truck' we say 'lorry', instead of 'elevator' we say 'lift' and instead of letting people die in the street, we have free healthcare." Ouch – but what was a playful slight from one comedian to another?

Russell also joked that he was "trying to fuck" Lady Gaga, although by the end of the night, he'd turned his attention back to the person he really wanted. "Katy Perry didn't win an award and she's staying at the same hotel as me, so she's gonna need a shoulder to cry on," Russell joked. "So in a way, I'm the real winner tonight."

His comments were laughed off as meaningless bravado but, at Lady Gaga's after-party that night, his prediction came true. Hedonism was in the air from the start, with Gaga dancing on the plush sofas and singing along loudly to her own songs. She might have faked being fatally wounded during her performance of 'Paparazzi', but – celebrating her aim – she was well and truly back from the dead. Amid all the chaos, tucked away in a corner, were Katy and Russell – and, according to eyewitnesses, they were passionately kissing.

The next day, after they parted, Russell sent his new beau a love poem and begged her to send one back. A woman of few words, Katy's response was simply to send a photograph of her bare breasts with the word 'POEM' written across them in lipstick. It hit the spot – Russell couldn't stop laughing.

Yet in spite of her overtures, if he was hoping to get into her underpants, he was to be bitterly disappointed. Katy might have been highly sexed and she might have been a tease but, knowing his reputation, she was giving away nothing. Instead, she demanded a dinner date, which was quickly followed by a spontaneous trip to Thailand. Although he was pulling out all the stops to romance her, she remained adamant that there would be no sex.

Posing as an amateur psychologist, Russell claimed he often manipulated women into intimacy, complimenting them. "Everyone inside them has a little self-doubt," he told *The Sun*. "If you help them to overcome that by recognising how beautiful they are, it's almost impossible for them not to have sex with you."

If his track record was anything to go by, his technique worked – but not with Katy. Supremely self-confident and sure of herself, she wasn't that easily swayed. At that stage in her career, she lacked self-doubt and needed no reassurance. She succeeded where Kate Moss had failed by not giving into the temptation of him. "Can you imagine the horrible feeling he had, when he was used to getting everything he wanted?" Katy asked *Esquire*.

Ironically, her hard-to-get demeanour made him want her all the more – sexual rejection was something of a novelty in Russell's world.

The two began officially dating, although there were some setbacks. The same day that Katy arrived in London to see him that October, he was reported to have been entertaining two women in his Hampstead flat. He clearly hadn't conquered his struggles with monogamy yet. In previous months, he'd promised every woman he'd started dating that he'd try to be faithful and that their influence in his life had "cured" his sex addiction, only to play away a couple of months later.

Given that he'd mentioned in *The Sun* that he would go through spells of being "deeply pious and celibate", before going back to his old ways, it became a well-worn chat-up line for women who had grown wary of his reputation. Could Katy really expect Britain's most notorious philanderer to stay true?

There were other differences between them that didn't bode well for their relationship either. Katy was no fan of casual encounters, whereas Russell was the king of them. She told *Complex* magazine that one-night stands were "disgusting", exclaiming, "Getting your flirt on is the best thing in the world, but when it comes to sharing your bodily fluids with a person you don't know, no thank you. Disgusting! Even if that's saliva, you know? Some people don't brush their teeth!"

Meanwhile Russell estimated that he'd slept with over 2,000 women. His flings had become so notorious in Britain that at one point *The Sun* had launched a hotline specially designed for his conquests to call in and spill the beans.

Even in LA, his reputation was known. Katy was accosted while shopping in one of her local haunts by a male fan who called over, "Have you and Russell gone and had STD tests together yet, or what? It's just the smart thing to do. There's a lot of things going round and your fella has been putting it about all over the place!"

Katy might have been seen as a hypocrite, first expressing her dislike for kissing random strangers and then publicly snogging someone who, in terms of saliva sharing, was the most notorious Lothario there was. Was she capable of handling the backlash?

Then there was the prospect of Russell as a parent. Katy had gushed that he'd be a "great baby daddy" but the only child Russell had ever practised his parenting skills on was his cat, who he joked was forever being told "Daddy's busy", while he went off to masturbate.

Then there was the small matter of Katy's parents, who expected her to marry a dutiful "man of God". As someone who saw himself as an atheist and regularly made religious jokes, Russell didn't exactly fit the bill.

On learning of the relationship, Katy's mother told *The Sun*: "How many times have your kids disappointed you so profoundly that you wanted to get up from the chair and knock them out?" Her response didn't seem in the spirit of Christianity, but she had clearly been inflamed by him, continuing: "This was a girl who wrote a song like 'Jesus Heals The Blind Eye'. She wrote songs like 'Faith Won't Fail' – and I am sticking that one in her face right now!"

Russell wasn't exactly an ideal son-in-law, even for the most liberal parents. He had suffered severe depression and suspected bipolar disorder since the age of 11. Throughout his teenage years, he had also flirted with bulimia, making himself sick in the sink on a daily basis. While this routine played itself out for three years, he didn't receive much in the way of support from his family. His stepfather's response? A curt request to stop blocking the drains with his vomit.

He replaced one bad habit with another when he began self-harming. His mother had been in remission from cancer, while his absent father – who had left the family home when he was a toddler – hadn't spent much time with Russell as he grew up. However, he once suggested that they reconnect with a trip to Thailand, where he had taken his son to partake in the pleasures of Bangkok's many brothels. Rumour abounded that he had lost his virginity to a prostitute, aided by his uncle.

This paved the way for Russell to begin a stint of womanising, enabled by his growing success as a young TV presenter and comedian. He was no stranger to drugs either, once claiming: "I started at 16 smoking stuff and drinking a lot. I started with loads of grass and hash, then took loads of amphetamines then loads of acid, loads of ecstasy and loads of coke, till in the end I took loads of crack and heroin." He'd even become addicted to the prescription drug Ritalin, like Katy's ex, Travis.

The next few years of his life were spent in a maelstrom of drugs, sex and rock 'n' roll. He'd even pleasured a gay man in the name of research for his comedy series and it seemed the only sexual perversion he hadn't succumbed to was paedophilia. Everything else – including extreme age-gap relationships and S&M – was featured on his provocative talk shows. Like the Sade song 'Smooth Operator' had warned, Russell was one of those tricky Western males, not for beginners or sensitive hearts – but maybe he was willing to change.

There had seemed no limits to his womanising – his last partner had caught him inviting girls to join in a threesome just after he sent her shopping with his mother – but Katy was hoping she could succeed where her rival had failed and successfully tame him. Secretly, she was enjoying the challenge.

The timing was perfect, as Katy's touring commitments were winding down for the year. Russell joined her in Paris in October for Fashion Week and they continued to develop their relationship there. If she'd been expecting flowers and chocolates though, she would have been disappointed – a romantic evening in Russell Brand's world involved a trip to the local cemetery.

The two visited the grave of singer Jim Morrison, whose rock star excesses had seen him drown in a bathtub. Could this have been a metaphor for the death of Russell's crazy lifestyle? Sure enough, he later tweeted: "I turned off my famous hedonistic hot tub... I did it for climate change. In every sense."

Meanwhile Katy had been gushing: "I'm in a love K-hole" on her Twitter account. In the clearest indication of their romance yet, Russell ended the speculation when he told a group of journalists outside his home that he'd fallen head over heels in love with her.

The pair were inseparable, with Russell even joining Katy in the studio. She had been scheduled to record ideas for a follow-up to *One Of The Boys*, but with her lover in tow, things didn't quite go to plan. He ended up reciting the 18th-century Edward Lear poem *The Owl And The Pussycat* into a microphone, while Katy belted out a chorus. "Russell was the owl because he's wise and, well, it's fairly obvious that Katy's a sex kitten, isn't it?" a source told *The Sun*.

However, not everyone was au fait with the romance. It even lost Katy the chance to be featured on the Gorillaz album *Plastic Beach*. Band member Murdoc Niccals told *BBC 6 Music*, "She's been after a guest spot for ages and I tried to turn her down. No, I couldn't work with the woman while she's got Russell Brand all over her." In an added slight directed at her new beau, he insisted: "I wouldn't work with anybody that I didn't admire."

Undeterred by his reaction, Katy introduced Russell to her favourite LA haunts, including the renowned nightclub H Wood. Once there, she and a female friend teased him with a sample of the titillating faux lesbian action that had got her into so much trouble already that year. Russell might have been waving a fond farewell to his hard-living past but, with Katy around, his future could never be boring.

On October 25, he joined her for her 25th birthday bash. The previous year, Katy had donned a moustache and dressed as Freddie Mercury, but this year the theme promised to be more girly and glamorous. Instructing all guests to wear white, Katy surprised them with a Charlie and The Chocolate Factory night, complete with candy and giant lollipops, and doused them in neon paint.

The Beach on Sunset restaurant in LA was transformed into Willy Wonka's famous factory for the night and guests including country star Taylor Swift emerged covered in food and paint. Russell tried to shield Katy from the cameras as they climbed into their getaway car, but the furious look on his face as he held up one arm covered with streaks of multicoloured paint was a hilarious sight. Even Perez Hilton approved, writing that the party had been "epic" on his blog the following day. Better still, the world hadn't seen the last of Katy's infamous candy theme – it wouldn't be reserved just for celebrity-studded parties by any means.

Meanwhile on November 5, Katy had been invited to host the European Music Awards in Berlin. She had decided to take some time out from her girly image, characterised by the fruit dress of 2008 and model herself on the musical *Cabaret* instead. The show she was emulating was more mature, sophisticated and seductive – and was based in the burlesque era of thirties Berlin.

"This year, the fruit has gone sour," she announced – it might well have done after a one-year absence and a destination change – "[and] it's darker, sexier, it's sultry, it's romantic – maybe with an undertone of S&M."

That promised to titillate a randy Russell. Yet the highlight for him was when she donned claret-and-blue-themed lingerie in the colours of his favourite football team, West Ham United. The outfit was produced entirely from the team's official shirts, but she had customised it by having her lover's nickname, Rusty, inscribed on the back of her pants.

A delighted Russell responded by promising to take her to a football match and he couldn't resist the opportunity for a wisecrack, tweeting: "No, I won't be taking her up the Arsenal!"

Russell then took over *The Sun's* entertainment column for the day, posting a photo of Katy in the Rusty pants with the quip: "A less dignified man might say, 'Not the first time I've decorated her bottom.'" Perhaps not the best way of endearing himself to the parents of the woman he wanted to marry, he continued by making a reference to her forthcoming *MTV Unplugged* video. "It will be magnificent but I wouldn't want people to think I was plugging her unplugged," he joked.

Similar chat had been a bone of contention between Katy's style icon, Dita Von Teese, and her ex Marilyn Manson, when she had begged him to stop making announcements about anal sex between the couple on the radio. But Katy forgave Russell's indiscretions – in fact, the pair were so wrapped up in each other that the normally career-focused Katy dropped a crucial radio show with Chris Moyles to be with him. She wanted to spend her final night in London with the man she loved.

What followed was the moment that Russ feared the most – meeting the family. After a few days of separation, he would fly to the Austrian ski resort of Ischgl, where Katy would be performing to celebrate the dawning of the winter season – and her parents would be there to inspect him.

He faced having to explain the endless sexual innuendos he'd made – and there was little point in denying them, as most of the jokes had been in public. "The first time I ever came against Russell was at the VMAs when he talked about my daughter's hole," her father Keith claimed later. "I didn't quite understand."

Meanwhile a nervous Russell was deep in conversation with her parents. "They're like refugees from the sixties," he told *The Guardian* of his first encounter with them. "They're really spiritual, take their religion seriously, but also he did do a lot of acid, her dad. He was born again as a result of almost being on the point of vagrancy." He added in awe: "Katy's mother went to Berkeley in San Francisco and went to a Doors gig and danced with Jimi Hendrix. They're not austerely judging me like Quakers, they really like me."

On hearing that Russell was doing his best to reform, her father Keith presented him with a copy of his book *The Cry*, an account of spiritual awakening and finding Jesus. Perhaps because he had once lived an out-of-control life, he knew where Russell was coming from. He also gave him a teddy bear with the words "When did my wild oats turn to bran?" written on the front. Inspired, Russell claimed, "The most important thing in my life now is recovery."

Katy also had some encouraging words for her reformed boyfriend. "He was a heroin addict and now he's not," she told *The Guardian*. "He was addicted to all kinds of things and now he's not. And he basically used to be a professional prostitute and now he's not." How did she feel about this transformation? "He's an extremist, which can be good and bad. I always needed someone stronger than me and I am, like, a fucking elephant of a woman."

Russell agreed with her admission, claiming that it was because she was so demanding that she was able to put him in his place. "I used to treat women badly, but I'm really trying my best," he told *The Mirror*. "There's no lying or tricking. It's a nice feeling... I love Katy in a really pure way. She's a beautiful person, funny, gentle and sweet. But she's so demanding. A lot of the time, it's mental. She's a proper handful. It's very diverting. It's easy to be an arsehole, but now I've a woman who won't tolerate it."

He went on to say that he'd mistaken his cravings to find the one and to be loved for lust – but in Katy he'd found what he'd been looking for. He'd plucked up the courage to tell Katy the full extent of his reputation, including allegations that he'd managed an entire harem of 10 girls, but she was undeterred. "What was really hard, the first few weeks I would say to Katy, 'You know I'm not seeing anyone else? I've stopped going on other dates?' And she'd be like, 'Yeah, that's good, so have I.' That's not enough praise!" he exclaimed to *The Sun*. "Here's the statistics of what I would have done in the last two weeks – look at that on a graph, the change in behaviour!"

Katy broke it to him then that she would always expect monogamy. "You have to be [faithful]," he continued, perhaps a little crestfallen. "That's one of the things about the institution of marriage. I've recently had that explained to me by my wife. You must be faithful. And I don't have a problem with that. I'm really, really in love..." So far, so good, until he added, "It's sort of odd, isn't it, because there is certainly a compromise.

You can't just maraud through life fucking whomever you'd like. Which is a shame cos I wish I actually could do that. That's the compromise."

His bare-bones honesty might not have been the romantic words Katy was hoping to hear, but Russell had no frame of reference for marriage. He'd lost the traditional family unit when his father left as a toddler and he'd lost his virginity to a prostitute. Yet, to his credit, he was taking on board the foreign concept of monogamy and trying to turn his life around.

For Katy, it was an ego boost to have ensnared a Lothario. She'd boasted about taming the "thug" that was her last boyfriend, Travis McCoy, and seemed to relish persuading a player to be her one and only. However, she'd truly fallen for him as well. In December, Russell was spotted shopping for a ring at a jeweller's, sparking rumours of the couple's engagement. Yet Katy proved how high-maintenance she could be when reports alleged that she wasn't satisfied with any of his choices and wanted a customised jewel designed for her.

Katy then returned the favour, proving she wasn't simply being mean-spirited, by buying her beau a Range Rover as a Christmas gift. Russell himself reciprocated by buying a multi-million dollar LA love nest close to Griffith Park.

Katy instantly set about putting her stamp on the place, converting the garage into a giant wardrobe and painting it pink. Perhaps she hadn't held out much hope that Russell would pass his forthcoming driving test and wanted to put the space to better use.

While Russell was evidently serious about Katy, the official marriage proposal did not come until a New Year break in India. The two had visited the Taj Mahal together and had matching tattoos inked on their inner arms reading "Go with the flow" in Sanskrit script.

They then travelled to Jaipur, checking into the lavish Rambagh Palace hotel. Quite what the exquisitely dressed, impeccably mannered staff at the former palace might have thought of Russell's brash honesty and bird's nest hairdo was uncertain – but they arranged a romantic meal in the gardens for them nonetheless.

Afterwards, they had their relationship blessed by a spiritual guru and, in an added twist, this was followed by watching a firework display from the back of an elephant.

Russell recalled of the special moment that almost went very wrong: "It's not a good idea to be on the back of an elephant during a fireworks display. They can't tell the difference between an apocalypse and New Year's Eve!"

It was then that Russell made his proposal – to a new start. He hid the long-awaited ring in a bouquet of flowers and, when she'd found it, asked her to be his bride.

Hollywood's most unlikely couple had just turned their relationship into a legendary love story. Russell's last ex-girlfriend had stepped out of the shadows warning that he would never change, but Katy's happiness didn't waver. Despite their differences, each had something the other lacked and needed in their life. Russell's edgy side intrigued her, whereas Katy's spiritual side – something of a rarity in Hollywood – was exactly what Russell had been yearning for to complete his recovery. Could they have met at just the right time?

Katy's father certainly seemed to think so. "We all have a past," he soothed. "He's got a real spiritual side [and] he has a whole new different concept on Christianity now that he has met her."

Plus her mother, who'd been dubious at first, was no longer worrying. "There are parts of Russell's book [autobiography *My Booky Wook*] where he's really hungry for positive influences in his life," she told *The Sun*. "The two of them are hungry. They're basically looking for God and seeking the truth – and they are going to find it."

Chapter 9

Living The Teenage Dream

Katy burst out of her love bubble to go back to work when she was invited to be a guest judge on *American Idol*. The TV show, fronted by Simon Cowell, gave hopeful singers a chance to show their skills and fight their way to a place in the music industry. Katy was delighted to be given the chance of mentoring and advising those who were auditioning – it was a little more glamorous than her early days working at Taxi, in any case. "If I was offered that job as a permanent host, I would ditch my career and take on that career!" she joked.

However, there was a dark side to her appearance. She knew all too well from her own experience how cut-throat the music business could be and, with that in mind, she pledged to be honest from the start, no matter how hurtful her words might be.

She introduced herself with the warning: "I've always been a brutally honest type of girl – don't ever put someone through because you feel bad." She also made no attempt to hide a feud between herself and judge Kara DioGuardi. The two had once been songwriting pals, but Katy was a little frostier on the show.

Young hopeful Chris Golightly came to the panel with a "sob story" – he'd been brought up in foster homes since he was 18 months old. He sang the Ben E King tune 'Stand By Me', which won the praise of other judges in the panel, especially Kara. "You're the kind of kid who has just enough talent and just enough of a story and pain and stuff that you've gone through in life to really connect with it and I think you're only going to get better," she told him.

Katy countered, "This is not a *Lifetime* movie, sweetheart. You have to have talent."

When the dust had settled, Kara got her revenge by mocking 'I Kissed A Girl'. Mortified by how Kara was "slaughtering" her song, she hissed, "Please stop before I throw my Coke in your face!"

Sensitive types might have been horrified, but for TV's own Mr. Nasty, Simon Cowell, her honest approach was appealing. Her insults even extended to him when she claimed: "As much as he's an arsehole, he's a very truthful, honest arsehole." He responded by saying: "She's definitely got her own opinion. She's a feisty solo artist and I like that."

Despite their catfight, Katy had given permission for an old song she'd written with Kara, 'I Do Not Hook Up', to be used on *American Idol* winner Kelly Clarkson's latest album. Just months earlier, in April 2009, her album had hit the shelves, also containing another of Katy's songs, 'Longshot'. Although it had been one of her rejects, it proved a hit for Kelly.

She got the chance to demonstrate her fearless, feisty persona again on the 30H!3 single, 'Starstrukk'. The video portrays the male band members fleeing from a group of angry girls who have had their coins stolen from a wishing fountain. The girls are both angry and athletic – not a good combination for the desperately fleeing group.

Meanwhile, Katy and her "daisy dukes" are portrayed as the object of everyone's desires, inspiring the group to look longingly at her as she sings with them in an LA rose garden. In the USA, the song peaked at a disappointing number 66 but, by January, it had climbed to number three in the UK – the highest ever chart position recorded for the group.

Katy enjoyed similar success with the single 'If We Ever Meet Again', released on February 15. She duetted with Timbaland, a producer turned frontman, for his album *Shock Value*. Her role in the video was to be his guardian angel, saving him from a self-destructive phase. "She saved my life with whatever depression I was going through, whether it be drug depression or weight-loss depression," Timbaland told MTV. "[The song asks] will she be around if I go through this again?" It pulled on the public's heart-strings in the UK, achieving a number three position in the charts and reached a peak of number 37 in the USA.

Katy's next major side project was to play Smurfette in an animated 3D film of *The Smurfs*. Producers invited her to take part after being seduced by the texture of her singing voice. "360 days out of the year, I feel like a cartoon," Katy told *MTV*, "so I thought playing a cartoon was a natural thing to do."

But there was one catch – bizarrely, the outwardly innocent children's cartoon encompassed everything that Katy's mother didn't want her daughter to be. In fact, as it was banned in her youth, the film would give Katy the opportunity to live a second childhood.

"I was never allowed to watch *The Smurfs*," she lamented. "Maybe it was very sorcery-based or magical or that Smurfette was the only female in the village – a slut, basically. Who knows?" Katy joked to *The Toronto Sun*. "But you can imagine how my mother felt when I called up and said, 'Hey, I'm Smurfette!'"

It was difficult to imagine what was more unusual – that her mother feared all things Smurf-related or that Katy felt taking on the role of a giant blue cartoon figure came naturally to her.

Perhaps to reassure her distressed mother, Katy insisted that there were no sexual innuendos this time. "This Smurfs is definitely one for the kids. It's not one of those movies that has to work on so many different levels," she told *The Daily Record*. "It's a family movie."

Katy also pleased her parents when she collaborated with the family-friendly Taylor Swift at her concert on April 15 at the LA Staples Center, the pair duetting on 'Hot And Cold'. She also showed her face at a string of annual award ceremonies including the Teen Choice Awards, where she dressed as a cheerleader with pom poms in a Smurfs shade of blue.

Katy had an impossibly hectic jet-setting schedule, but the most important thing for her over this period, besides romancing Russell, was recording her second album. This was the make-or-break album which she believed would prove whether she was truly talented or whether her success thus far had been a sheer fluke.

One of the first songs she worked on was 'Teenage Dream'. As Katy was about to marry and leave her single life behind for good, she wanted to look back on an era of her life that was drawing to a close and capture it on tape forever. Katy shared an obsession with Lolita with one of her co-writers, the flame-haired Bonnie McKee, and their material was inspired by that. The two of them had started out working at Katy's home town of Santa Barbara, which brought back sweet memories for her, while the album Bonnie had previously penned, *Confessions Of A Teenage Girl*, had left the awakening of youthful sexuality fresh in her mind.

The two began brainstorming with a lyric about Peter Pan and eternal youth, but later condemned it for lacking sexuality and edge. Less subtle lyrics joked about a girl who'd been caught up in the heat of the moment and had ended up "a mom in a mini-van". In Katy's Christian group of friends from childhood, condoms had been shunned as carrying them would imply that sex was premeditated. "No-one carries condoms and so they get pregnant the first time," Katy had told *Christianity Today*.

The two then experimented with sexual innuendos of "trying me on" under the guise of wearing new clothes. These ideas were inspired by Madonna's single 'Dress Me Up', which had hit the charts when Katy was just a year old. It was abandoned when the producers showed a lack of enthusiasm and asked them to base their song on a different single instead, 'Home Coming' by The Teenagers. That was when the pieces started to fall into place.

"I wrote that song in Santa Barbara and it was a very pure moment for me because that's where I'm from," Katy told *Celebuzz*. "It was, like, where I started my creative juices. Also, it kind of exudes this euphoric feeling because everybody remembers what their teenage dreams were – all the girls that were on your poster walls... and I want to continue to be one of those teenage wet dreams."

And who was Katy's personal teenage dream? While she was endlessly crushing on boys in her youth, her female fantasy had always been Gwen Stefani. "I still do idolise her," Katy told *MTV Asia*. "She's my be all and end all."

As the song fell into place, Katy captured an era of gleeful irresponsibility, one of addictive love. For her, it meant a time when all love affairs were pure and when heart ruled over head. She wanted it to capture the excitement of a first kiss, the thrill of "will we, won't we?" in early relationships and the untainted joy of love, before bad experiences caused cynicism.

"A lot of people fall in love for the first time and it's so intense and overwhelming and lovely in a way, but it's so emotional – but when you're an adult, you may not feel that way again," Katy told *The NZ Herald*. "The someone walks into your life who makes you feel that googly kind of love again." That person for Katy, of course, was Russell Brand.

There was a universal feeling of elation when the team finally nailed the song. "I couldn't believe after all of our agonising over youth themes that we had overlooked such an obvious one – the teenage condition," Bonnie sighed in relief. Meanwhile Max Martin, the same man who had relived Britney's first flushes of romance in 'Hit Me Baby One More Time', was feeling equally contented. He had sighed at the end, "I wish we could bottle this feeling!"

While Katy might have been satisfied with 'Teenage Dream', her work was far from over. The next track to take shape was 'Last Friday Night'. The song could easily have been the second episode of 'Waking Up In Vegas' with its tales of maxed-out credit cards, throbbing hangovers and one-night stands with strangers. Another common theme in both songs is that, while living large, Katy is deliriously happy.

The Hartford Courant tutted disapprovingly: "She glorifies getting wasted and misbehaving" – but it was merely an honest account of a young woman's life, complete with fond memories of her mishaps. In fact, it was based on a genuine night out in Santa Barbara. Everything, with the exception of the threesome, had really happened.

"It's just kinda about all those moments when you swear to God you're never going to mix Yager and lemon drop shots ever again, cos you feel like crap and then you do it all over again the next week," she told *The Dirt*. "I think it will go down well with college kids because they're always learning by default – by hangover – but they somehow can never stop!"

Yet while *Slant* magazine dismissed it as just another "trashy sorority party" soundtrack, there was more to it than that. While it seemed to be a superficially fun party-girl song, it also had hidden depths. Katy's reference to an "epic fail" reflects times when she drank to excess in her teens and had to face her family's disapproval. She had told *Blender* of that time in her life: "I started spending Sunday mornings crying and hung over, so my dad started telling me about when he was my age."

Clearly his tales of bad acid trips and drunken misadventures did little to deter Katy as she was re-embracing the party scene in a big way. But, during those early days, her father would reassure Katy and entertain her with stories of the mistakes of his own youth. As an attention-hungry middle child, the time she received from him during these moments was rewarding. Seeing Katy as a drunken mess seemed to appeal to his nurturing instinct and provoked the heart-to-hearts she'd always wanted.

In the song, childhood icons have turned twisted, with references to throwing a Barbie doll on the barbeque – a metaphor for her reckless loss of innocence. All of these factors combined gave 'Last Friday Night' the status of another song from the teenage era.

Meanwhile, 'Peacock' was inspired by a Nashville producer who taught Katy the art of songwriting when she was a beginner. He emphasised the importance of using metaphors and innuendos to add sparkle to a song – and Katy had taken his advice to heart.

"The person that was teaching me was an amazing songwriter and he was like, 'Don't forget about the double entendres. Don't forget about the puns. Don't forget that one word can have many meanings,'" Katy told *MTV*. "So I'm always kind of looking for that one thing that's really normal that you can make twisted." Little did the devoutly religious Nashville producer who had given her his well-intended advice know how she would go on to interpret it.

However, this song inspired a battle of wills between Katy and her record company. She had wanted to fight to make it a single, but its links to the male sex organ were seen as too controversial – so much so that Katy struggled to persuade them it had a place on the album at all. There was no fooling anyone that it was about a bird. Sure enough, there was a media backlash when it finally hit the shops, just as the label had predicted, with *Sputnik Music* claiming: "I would place money on

'Peacock' never seeing the light of day, primarily because it's a terrible song... so blunt it would make Ke$ha blush." *USA Today* even advised listeners to skip the song altogether.

Yet Katy defended to *The Music Mix*: "I'm hoping it will be a gay pride anthem. Peacocks represent a lot of individuality. It's not just the 'I wanna see your bulge.' It does have the word 'cock' in it, but 'art' is also in 'fart'. It's all in how you look at it."

She added "[My label] were all a bit worried about the word 'cock' and it gave me déjà vu because they did the exact same thing with 'I Kissed A Girl'. They said: 'We don't see it as a single, we don't want it on the album.' And I'm like, 'You guys are idiots.'"

Katy's instincts had paid off, as 'I Kissed A Girl' had sold in its millions. Plus Rihanna, one of Katy's best friends, had got the song 'Rude Boy' onto her latest album to an excellent reception, despite making similar explicit sexual references. Yet Katy's label remained cautious. She might have got 'I Kissed A Girl' through, but the battle with censorship hadn't ended just yet.

Undeterred, Katy continued with her vision, one that she hoped would be "an anthem for the go-go bars that gay boys will be singing at the top of their lungs".

Then there was 'Firework'. Some might have seen the track as another innuendo, but Katy had a different story to tell. She and Russell had been discussing her desire to die dramatically when that day came, by being shot in the ocean with fireworks. This reminded Russell of a passage from one of his favourite books, Jack Kerouac's travelogue *On The Road*. The passage read, "I want to be around people that are buzzing and fizzing all full of life and never say a commonplace thing. And they shoot across the sky like a firework making people go 'aww'."

Katy instantly related to the passage, telling *The Advocate*: "How poetic. I would love to make people go 'aww'." She incorporated that theme into her chorus.

Yet the most important message she wanted to give her fans was one of encouragement, urging that no matter how down they got, they should never forget the explosive potential within them. "It's hard to write an anthem that's not cheesy," she told *MTV*, "and I hope that this could be something in that category... one of those things where it's like, 'Yeah, I want to put my fist up and feel proud, feel strong.'"

Yet, as Katy had pointed out, even in her notoriously warm home state of California, it wasn't sunny every day. The songs 'Pearl' and 'The One That Got Away' demonstrated that. The latter expressed regret at a failed teenage romance with someone who remained close to Katy's heart. "It's having someone creep up on you that you dated from the past and feeling like they got away," she recalled.

Meanwhile, 'Pearl' is the tale of a woman who allows a relationship to cloud her brightness. Katy started writing the song about a fictional character, but halfway through she realised the song was autobiographical and that the character was her.

"Katy wanted to portray, 'Look, I'm a strong, confident woman but I succumb to these things sometimes too – you're not alone and no-one is invincible!'" a studio worker told the author. "It doesn't mean you're weak."

"It's the story of a person who changes because of a relationship. She was a pearl and now, she is just a shadow of herself because she let the other person destroy her," Katy elaborated to *Cool!* magazine. "I've been inspired by all the women who lose sight of who they really are because of their relationship. It happened to me too."

She added: "Since I finally found my soulmate, I began to think about all the boys I've been with in the past and wondered why I sacrificed a part of me for some of them when I could have used this time to grow up and get to know myself." This was a major problem in the early days, when Katy was still building her identity, as most of the men she dated were devout Christians who offered extensions of her parents' beliefs and her restrictive home life. It was when Katy met Russell that she felt she could finally be herself and enter a relationship that complemented her instead of swallowing her up.

The song 'E.T.' was an ode to that transformation. The metaphor of an alien portrayed the fact that his belief system was poles apart from the one she'd grown up with, but also nodded to the fact that she had fallen in love with a "foreigner".

The lyrics spoke of a cosmic kiss and Katy had earlier told *Cosmo Girl* that falling in love with Russell had been a "cosmic collision". The ambiguity of all that he represented to her was portrayed in the lyrics, "Could you be the devil, could you be an angel?" Meanwhile one verse, which discussed being led into the light, played back to her religious references.

'Hummingbird Heartbeat' was another ode to Russell and was Katy's answer to Madonna's 'Like A Virgin'. It discussed the feeling of losing her virginity each time her lover touched her. Monte Neuble, a co-writer, had grown up performing in churches as Katy had done and this added a new dimension to an otherwise saucy song.

'Who Am I Living For?' was the song Katy's Christian followers were longing for – one that dared to tackle the huge gulf between her raunchy stage antics and the relationship she insisted that she still had with God. Katy conceded that if her 15-year-old gospel singer self had met who she was now, she would have been "freaked", but it was that younger self who would relate the most to the song.

Metaphors such as bombs falling highlighted the repercussions Katy faced of living an alternative lifestyle and feeling like an outsider trapped between two cultures. To show how torn she felt trying to find the courage to pursue the forbidden fruit in her life, she portrayed herself as the Biblical character Esther.

In the Bible, Esther is depicted as the most beautiful woman in all the land. On account of her beauty, she is sent to the King of Persia for his hand in marriage, but she is hiding a secret that could see her persecuted – she is Jewish and an Israelite. When a law is passed that calls for all Israeli people to be put to death, Esther approaches the King, confesses, and asks for her life to be saved. He agrees and the man who passed the law is hanged. Her courage in making the decision to approach the King saves her life.

Katy spoke of needing God's strength to handle the pressure of making the breakthrough and have the courage to pursue her own dreams. Just as Esther would have been exiled from the Kingdom and murdered, Katy's desires to be different could have seen her turfed out from her family and church community. It was a big deal for her when God was once all she had ever known.

Katy explained the lyrics "Heavy is the head that wears the crown" by telling *E! Entertainment*: "When you wear a crown, sometimes it gets heavy and your neck hurts. I don't want people to be like, 'You're rich, you're famous, shut up!' I'm just trying to paint a picture that sometimes, when you're on a roller coaster, you don't like it and you freak out."

In fact, it was an ongoing battle for Katy, as she was still undecided about issues of right and wrong. She told *MTV Asia*: "I guess where I come from is still inside of me and nipping at my heels every day. It's interesting, along the road in the path of life, I meet a lot of different people who come from so many different places and they really influence and inspire who I am. I definitely continue to want to know the answers and have my own personal pilgrimage, so in a way it does affect what I do musically... one of the things that is most important in life is not collecting [awards] or trying to be as famous as possible, but to worry about your soul and your spirit and what's happening next."

Yet, according to Matthew Turner, she had no cause to worry for her soul. He told the author: "Did I sense conflict between her religious side and her wild side? No. The most beautiful part about Katy is her journey towards being completely real, authentic, honest. Every religious person has a wild side, but only the honest people ever allow that side to be revealed."

He added: "As with most of us, I think the tension is still there. Christianity isn't about one side winning or losing, it's about experiencing balance and I think that's something we're seeing Katy engage and wrestle with on that song."

Indeed, Katy spoke of seeing the heavens in front of her but being lured into the flames, insinuating that life was a constant battle between purity and decadence. It was one that she knew she had to express.

'Circle The Drain' was written about an ex-boyfriend's drug addiction and Katy's frustration in feeling that he loved substances more than he loved her. The song gave an account of her feelings of inadequacy when she couldn't change him and had to walk away. "It was intense," she told *The Age*. "I wanted to get things off my chest first before I could start clean and go to a sunny spot. It was stuck in my emotional filing cabinet for so long."

Using Alanis Morissette's 'You Oughta Know' – a reprimand to a lover who fails to live up to expectations – as her inspiration, Katy hit out that she wanted a lover, not a child who needed babying. The hapless lover she spoke of was none other than Travis McCoy, who had been addicted to Ritalin since the age of 15. When the pair had dated, Katy had invited him along to a Christmas show for the radio station X100 in New York, only to come off the stage and find he had been evicted from the venue for drug-fuelled mishaps.

For Katy, this was just one of her problems in the relationship and the song was a message urging him to clean up his act. Travis got his own back by releasing the phenomenally successful single 'Billionaire' about his desires to break free from his past and be wealthy and notorious. The song reached the top 20 in 17 countries and while it might not have made him a billionaire, he was finally back on the road to recovery.

In spite of this, Katy had no regrets, feeling that she had found her match in Russell. Using a fairy-tale framework to voice idealistic beliefs about love, Katy wanted to be like Snow White, waiting for her prince. 'Not Like The Movies' told of saying no to a fauxmance that didn't feel right and having enough self-respect to believe she deserved better. With Russell, another affair would make her feel like a charlatan, going through the motions in a meaningless relationship.

She confirmed to *Elle Canada*: "It's a snapshot of where I am. It's about love and heartbreak. As a woman, I feel like we get into a relationship, but we have this scratch inside that we don't pay attention to. You can tell this person isn't the one but feel, 'This is the best I can get. This is what I deserve.' My anthem on that song is to say I do believe there is a match out there for people. I started writing this song before I met Russell and I finished it afterwards. It's bittersweet in the beginning and it comes full circle."

While that might have been a positive note to end the album on, Katy was restless. She felt there was more she wanted to say. One night, she texted her A&R rep, Chris Anokute, to say: "Chris, I don't think my record is done. There is one more song I want to write, I feel it in my gut! I want to write a song about California girls!" He told *Hit Quarters*: "At the time the Jay-Z song 'Empire State Of Mind' was huge and everyone in LA was singing 'New York...' and she wanted to have a song for California. She had the whole vision!"

Katy concurred to *MTV Asia*: "I was hearing about 'Empire State Of Mind' and I was jealous! What about California? What about The Beach Boys? Or Tupac? I thought it would be time for a West Coast anthem with my twist."

She had an eclectic range of references, but most importantly she knew she'd need some established, home-grown talent to support her vision. She used Wikipedia to find out which Californian artists were all the rage in the music world and found Snoop Dogg.

"Instead of saying, 'Fuck you, I'm famous!', it's more like, 'No, I know my existence is reliant on these types of relationships and these people,'" Katy modestly told *The Toronto Sun*, "and that's why I'm inviting people out."

Katy worked Snoop Dogg into the lyrics, hoping some good old-fashioned flattery would persuade him to take part. "I started to insert Snoop Dogg references like 'sipping gin and juice' and more obvious ones like 'Snoop Doggy Dogg on the stereo,'" she explained. "And I was like, 'If Snoop Dogg was on a song about the West Coast, it would be truly legit!' So I kind of lured him with all these little odes to Snoop Dogg already in the lyrics!"

It all happened very quickly. Katy was in the studio working overtime to finish her vocal, when Chris contacted Snoop Dogg's manager, telling him the song would guarantee him a chance to get back on Top 40 radio. The track was so new that Chris didn't have so much as a demo to send, but Snoop agreed to come to the studio the same night on blind faith.

"I'm having dinner with my girlfriend and Ted calls me and says, 'Snoop's in town. If you're at the studio, we'll come now,'" he told *Hit Quarters*. "I get to the studio in a dash and Snoop beats me there. I see Katy Perry, Dr. Luke and Max Martin's faces and we look at each other like, 'Oh my God!' He listens to 'California Girls' and then rolls up some magic and 30 minutes later we're listening to 'California Girls' featuring Snoop!"

Katy fell in love with Snoop instantly. She told *The Toronto Sun*: "He is very West Coast. He's bullet-proof. He hung out with Tupac. He continues to impress the public because he's got so much versatility, from 'Drop It Like It's Hot' to his music video for 'Sensual Seduction' to letting us bury him in the sand [for the video]. He's still as cool as he was back in 'Gin And Juice'."

Even more importantly, Snoop had his own version of 'Waking Up In Vegas' – an earlier song called 'Signs' featuring Justin Timberlake. On the video, filmed at the legendary Palms Hotel, women cavorted on beds, writhing around with bank notes plastered over their bodies. The decadent theme suited Katy to a T and she knew she had wanted Snoop's participation at all costs. It was a nerve-racking task, but like Esther, she'd had the courage to track down the King of California – and it had paid off.

The veterans who were helping her now were not from the much-hated Nashville, but were California-born. "Can you imagine a Nashville Girls song full of crosses and Bibles?" an anonymous writer from Katy's past joked to the author. "There'd be no sex on the beach where we come from. But I'm glad that Katy had the courage to go for what she wants. It sounds like a hit."

At the filming, Katy lay naked in huge clouds of bubblegum-pink cotton candy. The theme had taken shape on the *One Of The Boys* tour, when Katy had wanted to create a Candyland atmosphere. She'd also experimented with the theme at her 25th birthday bash, where she'd handed out lollipops and candy galore. Now she was fulfilling her fantasy for real.

A blend of *Charlie And The Chocolate Factory*, *Alice In Wonderland* and the board game Candyland, the result is a fairy-tale fantasy world featuring ice creams, cupcakes, lollipops and giant game-board pieces. Snoop Dogg's role is the Sugar Daddy King and he has entrapped a harem full of Queens by luring them with candy and making them pawns in the game.

Perry liberates the women, who are then ambushed by Snoop's army of gummy bears. Katy wins again and, as a symbol of victory, places two guns of whipped cream on each breast, letting it squirt out at random. Snoop Dogg ends up buried under the sand, but the mischief doesn't quell his desire for the seductresses, as he wishes aloud that every woman could be from California. All of the backdrop

– from the Hollywood sign to the beaches – was made from real confectionery.

Katy was competitive and didn't want to be just another scantily clad pop starlet on a beach – she wanted to get creative. She told *The Toronto Sun*: "When you hear the song, you think, 'Girls on the beach, in bikinis and next to nothing', the same treatment you've seen for a lot of different music videos. I think it was just time to step up my game and the whipped–cream breasts were all a part of it."

Katy was filmed on the set of her video explaining with a demonic grin: "I decided to use my best assets, put some whipped cream on them, and spray those Gummy Bears!"

She even claimed that her video was "as innocent as Miley Cyrus", but while the pastel colours and candy might have given that impression, she knew it was tongue–in–cheek. "It's my favourite video that I got to make," she told *MTV Asia*. "I was eating real cotton candy and I was like, 'That's not work! That's play!'"

Snoop Dogg felt the same, although he implied that Katy owed the single's success to him. "I worked with Katy because she's a bad bitch but she needed a gangster to complete the deal," he told *Black Book*. "She had a cake with no candles on it, then she put me on 'California Girls' and it went straight to number one."

Critics might have argued that Katy had earned more number one singles in total than he had, but Katy felt that he was the "cherry on top" and that he had made her look "cooler". In fact, for California street cred, she believed there was no-one better to turn to.

The single was leaked to radio on May 6, leaving their plans for the promotional campaign in tatters. However, by the following day, it was number one in America as iTunes went on to sell 294,000 digital downloads in its first week. Seven weeks after it first hit radio, it made history by becoming the second-quickest-selling download ever made of a song. Its two million purchases put it close behind FloRida's 'Right Round' in the record books.

'California Girls' was like a speeded–up, funkier version of 'Teenage Dream' and it also resembled Ke$ha's 'Tik Tok', unsurprisingly, since Max Martin had been a co-writer behind all three tunes. It put Katy's alternative world, Candyland, on the map – and it was a serious contender to Alicia Keys' many songs about New York. For all of these reasons, the song soared in the charts.

Katy then landed a slot with Snoop Dogg at the MTV Movie Awards on June 6 – the perfect opportunity to premiere the song live. Lady Gaga had appeared in a raw meat dress that day, perhaps her answer to Katy's sushi and banana-themed outfits, but Katy wouldn't be upstaged. She started play by being suspended above the stage on a giant surfboard before coming down to earth alongside Snoop's virtual throne. She donned a Smurfs-style electric blue wig, glittery sequinned clothes and Gaga-style sunglasses for her debut, watched by thousands of Americans.

By now, people were drawing comparisons between Katy and Gaga for their religious backgrounds, their mutual desire to shock and provoke and their eccentric choices of outfits. In part, the media longed for them to be rivals and that month, the long-awaited moment arrived.

On June 8, Gaga's video 'Alejandro' hit TV. The same day, Katy posted a message on Twitter claiming, "Using blasphemy as entertainment is as cheap as a comedian telling a fart joke." The offending video featured Gaga dressed in a latex nun's habit, sucking provocatively on rosary beads and appearing with the symbol of the Holy Cross printed on her crotch. Could it be that seeing her chart rival clad in red latex and manipulating religion had inspired Katy's tweet?

She later told *Nylon* of Gaga's album, *The Fame Monster*, "When I first heard it, I was like, 'What the fuck is she talking about – teeth and 'he ate my heart' and monsters and 'dance in the dark' and shit? I thought she was such a shock jock."

Yet Katy had written songs depicting a love affair with God – was that not blasphemous too? Plus Katy had just as much of a reputation for shocking in her songs as Gaga had, and their outspoken attitudes were widely considered part of what had given them success. Would Katy, who by many accounts had turned her back on religion, be hypocritical to say what she had said? Did Katy simply fear Gaga's success and view her as a credible threat to her throne or was she genuinely affronted by the implications the song had for religion?

She told *Rolling Stone*: "I am sensitive to Russell taking the Lord's name in vain or to Lady Gaga putting a rosary in her mouth. I think when you put sex and spirituality in the same bottle and shake it up, bad things happen. Yes, I said I kissed a girl, but I didn't say it while fucking a crucifix." In the same feature, Katy had posed topless, with her hands cupped over her breasts.

She remained sensitive to religious slurs but eventually made up the feud with Gaga, telling *E! Online*: "The other day [Russell] was yelling out the window. He said something a bit off-colour, kind of blasphemous about the Lord Jesus Christ and I smacked him for it." She added, "It's just kind of deeply rooted inside me and hard to get away from. But everyone knows I am a massive Lady Gaga fan."

She added: "People say I'm a very hypocritical person [but] sexuality and spirituality are two separate things."

As for the turning point in Katy's love-hate relationship with Gaga, it was after watching the latter on the American Music Awards. She had a change of heart, telling *Nylon*: "I was like, 'You're an animal of another kind and we need you!'"

On June 14, Katy held a listening party in New York for her album. There was a beach theme and Katy arrived in implausibly high heels. "Ms Perry wasn't happy when she saw the small desert between her and her seat – 'I don't want sand in my stilettos!', she said, pouting, echoing one of her lyrics," *The New York Times* reported of the event. "But she is just a regular girl gone big, so she gamely tottered across the sand in her four-inch platforms, the heels disappearing at each step. Wearing flip-flops isn't really in the pop star playbook."

The following day, Katy was in Times Square, promoting her CD in a back-to-basics style. Singing from atop a Volkswagen, she made sexual gestures with her microphone to titillate curious passers-by. The album promotion was about to take off in a big way.

Just weeks earlier, she'd been living an ordinary life, relaxing and watching movies with her cats. Katy's OCD had taken a turn for the worse though, when she shaved her cat, Kitty Purry, totally bald aside from a single ring of fur around her neck. She had photographed her new look and posted guilt-ridden messages on Twitter asking, "My poor pussy, what have I done?" To add to her troubles, her OCD also meant that she was prone to panic attacks the instant she saw the hint of a fingerprint on a pair of sunglasses.

Her disorder didn't prevent her and Russell from buying a third cat however. "We have a new kitten called Krusty," she told *The Daily Record*. "We came up with it because it's Katy and Rusty, so crushed them together and made Krusty." The eight-week-old had been causing chaos with their sleeping patterns and putting Katy totally off the idea of pregnancy. "She is jumping on top of my head at 3 am and pissing in the bed and pooping in the bed. The whole works," she claimed. "Kids?! Ugh. This is a child, so I don't know if I can handle it right yet."

Yet she was willing to use pregnancy as a threat if her record label tried to work her too hard. She joked that she wanted the next album to feature her "barefoot and pregnant" to which her terrified publicist chimed in with, "Oh dear!"

Katy added to *The Daily Telegraph Australia*: "I do tell them, 'If you continue to push me harder, if you push me to the end, I'll get pregnant! I'll pull that card on you, so don't piss me off – I do have the power to have unprotected sex, you know!'" To Katy's label, she was unpredictable and dangerous – a firework waiting to go off.

Family life might have been idyllic with Russell and the cats, but it was time to get back on the road. On June 28, she made a surprise appearance on *The X-Factor*, standing in for Australian judge Dannii Minogue, who, ironically, was taking time off as she was pregnant.

At the Dublin auditions, Katy's steely exterior and refusal to be seduced by "sob stories" put her in good stead for winning Simon Cowell's affections. She made her position clear when she strode on stage with the battle-cry, "Today we're going to give Simon a taste of his own medicine!"

Following *The X-Factor*, Katy made the controversial decision to pose nude for the first time ever in the name of art for her album cover. She had first met artist Will Cotton, who shared her passion for Candyland scenes, after she had made an enquiry about purchasing some of his paintings. Shuddering at the price tag, she was a little relieved to learn that her favourites had already been sold, but they had common ground.

Will emailed her back asking, "Is that Katy Perry the singer?" and the communication that followed sparked a meeting of minds.

"Before I even discovered Will, I was into all things cute and girly and beautiful and edible," Katy told *ArtInfo*. "[I admire] Will's ability to capture the beauty of a woman and not in some kind of kitsch, annoying, obnoxious way, but really just in a gorgeous, beautiful, totally twisted way."

Will already secretly had a collection of photos of her which had inspired some of his work, so he was delighted to hear that the appreciation was mutual. "The reason I chose Katy and no-one else [as a muse] – I had torn pictures of her out of magazines, because she was just the kind of character that I wanted to paint," Will told *The Daily Beast*. "She's very over the top, she's very sugary, saccharine, as sweet as can be."

Like many renowned artists, there was a division of opinion about his work. Critics claimed that the naked Venus-style paintings of girls which had caught Katy's eye were "demeaning". Will, on the other hand, thought his work was playful and "celebratory". Katy felt the same – and once they understood this, they were keen to work together.

Will had started off as an art director on 'California Girls', which had received an awe-inspiring 100 million hits on Youtube. The album cover seemed a natural progression. "This was a super-professional operation – literally, three hours of hair and make-up just to get ready to pose for a painting," Will recalled. Katy had allegedly applied her own make-up, however. Will then made several paintings for consideration for the cover.

"[For one] I made a painting of the scene with Katy licking an ice-cream cone in a taffy forest," he explained. "For the dress, I took shiny foil cupcake papers. I was over at [designer] Cynthia Rowley's house and she has daughters and they have Barbie dolls. So I cut out the cupcake papers, I put them on a Barbie and I said, 'Cynthia, could you possibly make this dress?'" She was happy to oblige and on the day of the shoot, the papers were sewn directly onto Katy.

Being with the man she loved had given her extra body-confidence and she had no hesitation about unveiling all for photos she knew would be plastered across billboards all over the world.

Yet the one issue she did struggle with was kissing another man on the video shoot for forthcoming single 'Teenage Dream'. The director had cast a love interest that matched Katy's euphoric promises of dancing until she died. The song had the youthful optimism of a tune like 'Get What You Give' by The New Radicals, which also recalled teenage mischief, and it was up to Katy's team to make that emotion come across on camera.

Katy drove in an open-back car, throwing her arms in the air before embracing model Josh Kloss in a hotel swimming pool. "I had to make out with a boy, which was very traumatising [because I'm in love] so I was kinda mean to him," she recalled. "I would be the one to call cut because I was like, 'Oh, I can't do this!' I feel so horrible, but I know it's a job. Russell and I understand what our work is."

The other trauma was that, owing to the lyric about a boyfriend who idolises her even with no make-up on, she was almost bare-skinned in the video. For a woman who modelled herself on drag queens and would insist "None of this natural nonsense!" when make-up artists were working on her, this facial deflowering was a challenge.

"You'll see a very raw, almost vulnerable side to me. I had to wear so many less layers of make-up," she winced.

Listeners were totally undeterred and, on July 23, the day it was released, it sold 55,000 copies via iTunes. Even more thrilling for Katy was the news that she had broken the first-day sales record for highest number of downloads – an accolade previously held by rival song 'Empire State Of Mind'. California girls really had got the upper hand.

Soon after that, it climbed to number one on the US Billboard chart, after receiving 14.4 million radio plays across the country. The single went on to sell more than three million copies.

Katy's elation was interrupted by a nasty surprise – The Beach Boys' record label was planning to sue Katy and claim royalties for the lyric "I wish they could all be California girls!" sung by Snoop Dogg.

However, she took the bad news in her stride. "To be on Brian Wilson's radar is probably as big as to be on Queen's radar. I love them!" she exclaimed. Meanwhile, the band claimed that they had loved the song, were flattered to have inspired it and knew nothing of the plans to sue.

Yet Katy wasn't just taking ideas from others – she was inspiring people herself. On August 23, she played at London's O2 Arena wearing her electric blue Smurfs wig and smothered in neon green paint. The look was an acquired taste but it appealed to young hopeful Selena Gomez, a former child actress who was now in music.

Although Selena had been raised in a strict Catholic family and wore a purity ring, Katy's exhibitionism was right up her street. She announced to *Z100*: "I'm going to be Katy Perry for Halloween. I'm gonna have the blue wig and a blue dress with ice cream on it and candy-cane shoes." Lest it was mistaken for a back-handed compliment, she added, "I was, like, star-struck by her. She's so amazing and one of my inspirations."

Katy had also given her the song 'Rock God' for her album *A Year Without Rain*. "I actually had to fight for that song," she recalled. "I wanted it so bad." Katy contributed backing vocals to the re-recording to put her stamp on the track and Selena had felt "very blessed" to have shared the studio with her.

Meanwhile Katy was focusing on her own album, which had an August 24 release. She had boasted that it was the sound of summer, channelling hot dogs, inline skating and the obligatory cotton candy. She joked to *The Daily Telegraph Australia*: "I'm not saying the whole record is going to be a bunch of sugar – I don't want to make people diabetic or anything. I want to fill their complete appetite with the record, I think, as they dive in deeper. [That] kinda happened with *One of the Boys*. You were fully satisfied – it wasn't all sugary sweet." Her fans agreed. The album debuted at number one in the USA, Canada, Australia and the UK.

As part of promotion, Katy had the opportunity to go back to her former high school, Dos Pueblos, for an extra-special show. She might have outgrown playing to small audiences, but when she took to the stage on September 14, it was the most glamorous school reunion she could have hoped for. She also relished the chance to mock and humiliate a love interest who had spurned her all those years before. "Is that Shane Lopes?" she bellowed into the microphone. "You were the most popular kid in my class, but you never wanted to date me. Oh yeah, you really chose well. What's up now, player? I dedicate this next one to Shane Lopes... it's called 'Ur So Gay'." Katy had got the ultimate revenge.

Not only that, but she knew her sex appeal was working when she became too hot for television. She had been invited onto the children's TV show *Sesame Street* to sing 'Hot And Cold' with the lovable cartoon character Elmo. In the clip, she had chased him around, changing the words of the song to, "You're up and you're down, you're running around, you're fast then you're slow, you stop then you go."

However, the clip was abruptly pulled when her cleavage upstaged Elmo. Underneath a revealing dress, Katy was wearing a flesh-coloured mesh top for modesty, but furious parents deemed it inappropriate, logging on to the Internet to make a record number of complaints. One woman claimed her young son had his first erection while watching the clip. Other complaints included, "You can practically see her tits. That's some wonderful children's programming!", "They're gonna have to rename it Cleavage Avenue!" and, "My kid wants milk now!"

Some comments were certainly tongue-in-cheek, but the embarrassed programmers delegated the video to Youtube and banned it from the televised show. As for Katy, she took all the fun as a compliment.

Katy's fame was now growing by the day. With her album release and her high-profile relationship with Russell, she was hot property – and the media attention had become more overwhelming than ever before. The pressure came to a head one September morning when the couple disembarked from a flight in Los Angeles to be greeted by a sea of press photographers. Russell was so enraged when he caught one allegedly aiming a lens up his fiancée's skirt that he punched him, and was promptly arrested. Katy defended his reaction on Twitter, saying he was merely "doing his job" by protecting her.

However, the turbulent relationship with the paparazzi also had its upside. Katy found herself trading photo opportunities for spare change for the parking meter. "I was running late, so I was like, 'OK, I'm essentially paying you, so could you put 50 cents in the meter?'" Katy joked to *Nylon*.

She summed up the problem with the words: "They're good and they're bad. If they're not there, then obviously it's not working in your favour. If they're there, you want them gone. It's a catch 22. Russell is in the same headspace."

The relationship between the couple was attracting so much attention that, in the interest of maintaining professionalism, a decision was made to cut their kissing scene from *Get Him To The Greek*. The pair were concerned that what the film had to offer would be overshadowed by the coverage of their first kiss – something that was now too private to share. The romance might have been "just like the movies" but they couldn't let the movies overlap with real life and they needed to keep a hold on what was real. "There is a place to be professional and a place to be intimate," Katy told *The Express*, "and sometimes they can't co-exist."

That was the case for the pair's forthcoming nuptials – something which they hoped would be the biggest secret of all.

Chapter 10

Fireworks, Cupcakes
And Cotton Candy

This was no ordinary celebrity wedding. Shunning the multi-million pound photo shoots and glossy magazine covers, the two wanted their special day to be theirs alone.

"We just love each other and we want to get married in front of our friends and family and keep it very normal," Russell claimed. "It ain't about selling the pictures, it ain't about doing no pre-nup, it's just a normal thing. I'm trying to preserve it, to keep it a beautiful thing. I think people get the wrong idea about how we want the wedding to play out. Love between two people is the most beautiful thing in the world."

Two of the celebrity world's biggest exhibitionists were stepping out of the limelight by choice. Of course, that didn't stop the playful public banter between them from increasing as the day grew near.

Russell told a US radio station: "Katy, that little cow, keeps calling me a bridezilla." She had fabricated the rumour as a joke, but Russell was determined to get his own back, claiming, "I'm trying to think of a way to get revenge. There are photos of her on my phone that could go nuclear, but a man has to be respectful."

When offered the opportunity to splash them across every news network in the country, he declined, insisting: "I'm so tempted, but I feel I'm going to need my testicles for the future!"

However, he did get his revenge eventually, posting a photograph of a bare-faced, make-up-free Katy on his Twitter account. She was mortified, despite looking radiant, and vowed to plan her own revenge.

Although the stream of jokes remained constant, the wedding itself was shrouded in secrecy. In fact, the couple were so eager to preserve their privacy that, when the big day came on October 23, they fled from the prying eyes of the media and returned to India.

The lavish, ultra-private reception was held at the Aman-i-Khás hotel, close to Ranthambore's tiger sanctuary, and allegedly included a parade of 21 elephants, camels and horses. The only unwanted guest was India's very own killer queen – a female tiger on a murderous rampage. The tiger, which had killed three locals already that year, was seduced by the sounds of the party – or perhaps it just wanted a dance with the bride-to-be. Fortunately, the guests escaped its hungry jaws.

Although the wedding was traditional, conducted by a Christian minister at the request of Katy's parents, some aspects were less conventional. Katy's best friend, gay fashion designer Markus Molinari, was a bridesmaid – just as he had been in the 'Hot And Cold' video. Before the ceremony she threatened to make him wear "one of those horrible Jessica McClintock dresses, for sure!" This would cater to Katy's drag-queen fantasies. She'd watched every single episode of *Ru Paul's Drag Race* and was raring to go with dressing her male friends the same way.

Her other gay guests included stylist Johnny Wujek and her manager Bradford Cobb, meaning she was surrounded by the very people she was often accused of discriminating against. If Katy had ever felt prejudice about homosexuals, she had since been forced to reconsider, as these were the very people that had shaped her career.

Katy had imposed a ban on sex before marriage – perhaps she was afraid she'd be jilted at the altar otherwise, just as her virtual boyfriend in 'Hot And Cold' had done – but she had ensured her own mood swings on the wedding night would be much easier to decipher. She'd invested in an emotionally activated lip-gloss by Too Faced, which turns from a sheer pink sheen to a deep crimson to alert a partner when the wearer is in the mood for love.

There were even stories that the pair had taken to trading their jewellery at the ceremony. According to Katy, her lover had one of the largest collections she'd ever seen, but hopefully he escaped any taunts of 'You're so gay' on the night. Meanwhile, the most cherished pieces of jewellery the pair would trade were rings, as they became man and wife.

Three days later, Katy's latest single, 'Firework', launched. The message was simple. Video director Dave Meyers explained: "We wanted to articulate the meaning of that song: what it means to be an underdog and have the courage, if you're on the outskirts of society, to be your own person."

That message meant more to Katy than an onlooker might have guessed. Now that she was in a position of strength and euphoria in her career and was delighted with her love life, she wanted to encourage her fans to embody that emotional strength and self-confidence too.

Yet it hadn't always been that way – her route to fame had been long and rocky and her own failures were recent enough for her to appreciate what taking the role of underdog felt like. "[I felt like] one big fat fail," Katy had told *The Chron* after finally making it. "[Success] feels like a release, like I've been holding my breath underwater. You're at the bottom of that pool and you know you're going to die. Your brain's frying and you come up for air... it's almost like a life-or-death thing."

Knowing this, Katy didn't want to come across as an unreachable, cooler-than-thou pop star. She wanted to write about real life – and she hadn't always been that desirable killer queen. She'd never had financial backing from wealthy parents either – just raw ambition and blind faith.

'Firework' was a metaphor for Katy's explosion into the pop world, and she wanted others to take heart from that message and give birth to their own brightly coloured fireworks. The video portrays a lonely, awkward, gay teenager struggling to come to terms with his sexuality, who finally plucks up the courage to kiss his male friend, throwing caution to the winds to admit who he is. Meanwhile, a bald-headed child victim of leukaemia sits forlornly on a hospital bed, embarrassed about her looks, before breaking free of her restraints and walking through the streets with pride. A trainee magician battles with muggers not through violence, but through magic tricks. An overweight young woman stands at the sidelines of a party before finding the confidence to join the others, jumping defiantly into the swimming pool. The centrepiece of the scene is Katy, who sees everything from her vantage point atop the balcony of Buda Castle in the Hungarian capital. As she sings, fireworks cascade from her chest. She is telling viewers what she told herself in her darkest moments – never to give up.

It was Katy's idea to unleash fireworks from her breasts, taking things a step further from the whipped cream that had exploded from them in 'California Girls'. The act also closely resembled a part of Lady Gaga's stage show. Whether consciously or not, Gaga and Katy often seemed to battle to outdo each other in the outrageousness stakes. When Katy wore a deck of cards in her hair, Gaga wove drinks cans into hers. Both wore food-themed dresses to award ceremonies. Both sang bi-curious anthems with contagious beats – and now, both would explode fireworks from their chests.

Director Dave Meyers was keen to use real fireworks but met serious opposition for health and safety reasons. "I tried to figure out a way to actually rig real fireworks to real people," he recalled, "but it ended up being a hazard. Nobody wanted me to get close to Katy with them."

While the fireworks might not have been real, the actors – just like the message – definitely were. As Katy had been writing with ordinary people in mind, she wanted the characters to reflect that by shunning Hollywood concepts of perfection.

Finding two men in the notoriously homophobic city of Budapest who were willing to admit that they were gay had been a challenge, but Dave managed to find a genuine couple. He also found a young fan willing to shave her head to be in the video. "[She] isn't actually a sick girl, but we got her to shave her head and, if you're an 11-year-old, that's a massive commitment," Dave recalled. "The people's commitment to it was really beautiful." He even managed to find 250 fans to act as extras. "That was 250 hardcore Katy Perry fans," he explained. "Those people were jumping [in the video] because they were loving life."

The newly crowned Mrs Brand was loving life, too. In November 2010, she was touring the world to unveil her new perfume, Purr. The publicity shots saw Katy pose on all fours in a skintight pink and purple latex catsuit adorned with black leopard spots and complete with a matching tail. She teasingly pawed at a giant ball of wool that was bigger than her own head. Even the bottle, shaped as a cat, took on a feline theme. Inside was a fruity-floral fragrance, featuring notes of rose, vanilla, sandalwood, apple and peach. Katy was keen to continue the theme by being a sex kitten herself, promoting her perfume all over the world in a variety of scantily clad outfits.

She also began planning the video for forthcoming single 'E.T.' Not only had she secured Kanye West to provide some rap vocals, but she had decided to dress herself as an alien, too. "'E.T.' is a metaphor about finding someone who is just obviously not from this world, because how could they love me like this?" Katy explained to *Company*. It contradicted her religious faith, but Katy had turned out to be a strong believer in alternative life-forms, adding, "I look out into the sky and I feel like there is so much out there... I'm interested in all things futuristic."

In fact, she even believed that her relationship with Russell had been written in the stars.

However, her life took on a softer, more traditional pace at the 2011 Grammy awards on February 13. Katy arrived with her grandmother, joking, "If I don't go home with any Grammys, at least I go home with my grammy."

She then performed 'Not Like The Movies' alongside video footage of her and Russell exchanging their marriage vows and their first kiss as man and wife. Although she left without scooping a Grammy from her four nominations, she was happy just to have had a memorable night with her loved ones. Perhaps there was a "girl next door" side to Katy after all.

Russ Breimeier mused: "[Katy is] pretty consistent in [her] focus on partying, drinking and sex [but] the sad part is you can tell from a few songs that there's a more rational girl next door under the wild exterior."

Yet Katy had defiantly told *The Scotsman*: "I tell all the colours of the rainbow, not just the pink ones."

She was determined to be frank, honest and outspoken, leaving little to the imagination, and yet in spite of her unshielded honesty, she was still a bundle of contradictions.

Some preferred to see her as the God-fearing girl of old. Russ told the author: "People have mocked me for this, thinking I'm naive, but I still hold out hope that Katy may come around one day and embrace her faith more closely."

Like Russ, Katy's parents were desperate to change her, insisting at one of their church services: "She knows where she is supposed to be and she will return. There *is* a battle going on for her soul, as there are for millions of other young people not being able to figure out homosexuality, fornication and other religions. That's mainly because they put down their Bible and stopped attending church."

Katy was guilty as charged. However, according to her father, after a night of singing about sex and flashing her underwear to a 10,000-strong crowd, she could still occasionally be found huddled in her dressing room reading her Bible.

What was more, after a raunchy photo-shoot with a magazine, she had gazed at her Jesus tattoo and remarked: "That's where I come from and that's probably where I'll go back to."

That was the tease about Katy – who was she? It was a tale of two Katys, from the angelic, blond teenage girl reading her Bible, her hands clasped earnestly in prayer, to the raven-haired scantily clad, Lolita-like sex symbol with a twinkle in her eye. Her appearance had changed, her sound had changed, but who was she inside?

In 'E.T.', she questioned whether a mystery man was an angel or the devil in disguise, but she could just as easily have been referring to herself – and her Lolita image of twisted innocence allowed her to play both roles at the same time.

Even her tour was filled with contradictions. Underneath her child-like smile, there was a desire for world domination, one candy town at a time. While Katy had promised her spring 2011 tour would be a little darker and "less cute", she had ended up with a stage show just as kitsch as ever, striding onstage in a dress dotted with miniature cupcakes.

She had kept her pledge to be forever young though, promising her fans edible confetti and up to 20 outfit changes per night. As viewers of her March 17 show at London's Hammersmith Apollo discovered, this was no cheap publicity stunt. True to her word, even the air was scented with her signature flavours of cotton candy and cherry chapstick. It was also tinged, of course, with the odour of sweat in a venue packed full to capacity, or − for the more refined fans − a spritz of her new fragrance, Purr.

It wasn't just the perfumed girls who were eager for a glimpse of Katy's show either. According to one review, men in the crowd were audibly expressing their desire to "get a load of her massive cupcakes", before turning uncharacteristically quiet as they too were genuinely drawn into her sugar-coated world.

Katy was a veritable hypnotist. Formerly macho men and sensible business types alike were giving in to temptation. Even *The Financial Times*, which ordinarily played it safe, was seduced by her surrealist candyland tour and its "forbidden pleasures". Its reviewer claimed Katy's performance was "colourful, theatrical and entertaining".

It was a multicultural tour, too. Not only was her own brand of California cool radiating through the air, but her stage show also resembled a good old-fashioned German fairy tale − a girl searching for her lost cat and getting into harm's way *Hansel And Gretel* style, before finding her love match in the shape of a tasty gingerbread man. Yet the world was a dangerous place for a girl who could have been Snow White's identical twin when wicked witches and evil butchers lurked around every corner, not to mention mime artists haranguing her for a peek up her dress.

Added to this slightly sinister fairy story was the burlesque vibe of thirties Shanghai, a touch of Alice in Acidland and the look of a Parisian cabaret dancer straight from the Moulin Rouge.

The transformation was aided by her many outfit changes − six in 'Hot And Cold' alone − but it was the image of a Las Vegas showgirl that she lived up to the most. In fact, she seemed the picture of elegance in her heart-shaped, crimson-coloured, rhinestone-encrusted corset and billowing pastel-pink cotton candy-style tutu − until her husband's influence added a range of brash Essex references to her repertoire.

Katy revealed to the audience that she had been introduced to English TV by Russell and now counted *The Only Way Is Essex* and *My Big Fat Gypsy Wedding* among her favourites. Seasoned Londoners audibly groaned. It was the dark side of the fairy tale – an innocence that had been ever so slightly hackneyed around the edges.

The diversity of the show was also apparent in her song choices, when she covered a range of tunes from the hard-edged Jay Z's 'Big Pimpin'' (how might he have reacted to all the pink?) to her friend Rihanna's 'Only Girl In The World' and Whitney Houston's 'I Wanna Dance With Somebody'. Finally she cultivated her love-hate relationship with Lady Gaga by sampling her own version of her rival's single 'Born This Way'.

Meanwhile, lovably ludicrous props included a Dita Von Teese inspired swing, a candy-cane staircase, dancing gingerbread men and a rhinestone-smothered flute, which she confessed – as it fell apart – that she had no idea how to play.

Her quirky stage show impressed and the positive reviews came pouring in. *The Daily Telegraph* was particularly complimentary, hailing her "megawatt jukebox musical" as a "show to satisfy the sweetest tooth". As reviewers joked that they had left with a serious sugar addiction and the urge to find the nearest bakery for a slice of "Perry pie", Katy was preparing to preach her forbidden fruitcake to yet another city.

As the tour continued, no-one could doubt that she was different and she certainly wasn't predictable. She would be the firework she sang about – bright, beautiful and ever so slightly dangerous – something that fans could admire from afar provided that they stood back in the wake of the explosion.

Yet the question of who Katy was remained – is she really the repressed ex-choir girl longing to break free from the chains of a sheltered childhood, or is she simply sexing up her image to shock because – as previous attempts at success suggested – it was the only way back then of getting attention on a mass scale?

Is Katy a religious zealot, a visual prostitute, or a puzzling mixture of the two? And, as increasingly outrageous stories sweep the web about the volatile state of her marriage, will Katy become debauched as Russell was? Will Russell find a spiritual side through her? Or will there be a balance between the two?

Whatever her truth, she's selling sex, songs and sensationalism and, given her enormous success so far, that looks set to continue for a long time to come.